Case Studies in Public Sector Procurement and Design

Case Studies in Public Sector Procurement and Design

Alexis D Brooks MSc.d. MCIPS

Published by Liverpool Business Publishing
an imprint of
Liverpool Academic Press

© Alexis D Brooks 2002

First published in Great Britain by Liverpool Business Publishing

A CIP catalogue for this book is available from the British Library

ISBN 1 903500 09 5

The right of the author of this work has been asserted by her in accordance with the Copyright, Designs and Patents Act 1988.

All rights reserved. No part of this publication may be reproduced, stored in a retrieval system, or transmitted in any form or by any means, electronic, mechanical, photocopying, recording, or otherwise without prior permission of Liverpool Business Publishing, 12, Caldbeck Road, Croft Business Park, Bromborough, Wirral, CH62 3PL.

Typeset by Bitter & Twisted, N. Wales

Printed and Bound in Great Britain by Lightning Source UK Ltd, Milton Keynes.

"I dedicate this book to my mother Hazel
and to my sister Marcia for their love and support in my life;
to my special cousins Ann and Stanley Smith,
and to my father John Alexander Brooks, God rest him,
without whose love, drive and spirit
I would not be where I am today."

Foreword

Design at its best isn't just about the way things look and feel. Successful businesses, for instance, see it as a way of working and of creating the systems which turn ideas into tangible products and services that connect with customers and anticipate their needs.

It can be just the same for the public sector. Using good design can help with measures like changing a government department's corporate identity or decorating its office, but it can also transform the processes behind the development and delivery of policies and services so that they meet people's needs effectively in a way that delivers good value for money.

And with delivery firmly at the top of the Government agenda, that's something more worthy than ever of serious investigation.

The case studies presented here provide great examples of how procurement processes can benefit from design thinking and design management, and I am delighted that the Design Council is helping to make them available.

Andrew Summers
CHIEF EXECUTIVE
DESIGN COUNCIL

Case Studies in Public Sector Procurement and Design

Contents

Chapter 1	Procurement in the Public Sector - best practice process using design factors	1
Chapter 2	Inland Revenue case study	8
Chapter 3	Belfast City Council case study - Café at the crematorium	31
Chapter 4	Government purchasing card case study	50
Chapter 5	Driving Standards Agency driving test theory case study	66
Chapter 6	Driver and Vehicle Licensing Agency case study	91
Chapter 7	Local authority procurement of waste management	113
	Companion lecturers' aid for public sector design case studies	128

Chapter 1

Procurement in the Public Sector - Best Practice Process Using Design Factors

Introduction

'Design has a central role to play in the total process of achieving value for money in the delivery of government services.' (*Brian Rigby, Director Treasury Procurement Group, 1999*).

Central Government in Britain spends in the region of £24 billion a year on goods and services. This presents a massive opportunity to incorporate innovation and design into the many and various lines of procurements undertaken in the sector.

In the context of this research we are concerned with 'Design' of products and services for utilisation within the public sector business activity. In general terms we tend to think of product as a tangible physical object like a piece of furniture or a storage cabinet. A service implies a more tangible experience such as security, cleaning or a training event. A product or service is anything that can be offered to customers in order to satisfy their needs and expectations. There are three levels relating to such satisfaction: those of expected benefits that the customer is buying, the component products and services that are bought and the processes gone through to achieve delivery. The process is vitally important, as it is this operation that creates the products and services, puts them together into packages and delivers them to the customer to fulfil the need. Design is the key to all of this.

Thirty years ago the image of design was viewed in one of three ways: as irrelevant, as a dominant styling criterion, or as a key criterion that followed function (Desbarets 1995). 'Design is changing ...it is the thinking that's changing the forms of our living and this thinking is changing all the time.' (Jones 1990). At one time designing was done in amongst making and using the product. It was seen very much as a craft. Design then was made into a job of its own, identifying it as a specialism and segregating it from other activities in business. In doing so this has affected the ability of individuals and disciplines to see the entire picture pertaining to product and service development and utilisation and the management of the wider supply chain. Each discipline or function, i.e. procurement, design, etc, has removed itself into its own world and therefore fails to take account of each other's perspective and of many factors affecting the wider picture. Each function or discipline relies on its own models and processes which does not help in the visualisation of the product, identification of need, nor the wider concerns about the product development such as cost, availability of sources of supply, fitness for purpose nor affordability of materials or components. It is design of a product which determines its whole life cost, i.e. how much maintenance it needs, how much energy it uses, how long it lasts and how much staff time it takes to use it. Using design to achieve total value for money therefore instead of focusing purely on the purchase price would have significant impact on the costs of government (Rigby 1999). There needs to be attention given to product and service design and the relationships between various stakeholders in the visualisation and actualisation of products and services in the business context. It is important to enhance understanding and thereby add value, through exchanges internal and external to the organisation through the procurement process, as it is here that many of the above issues can be affected.

Pugh (1991) believes that all design should start from the identification of user need and that when this is satisfied the product will fit into the required environment. Underpinning this belief is the need to develop a 'product brief' or product specification. Many 'stakeholders' and factors are involved in the development of this specification. Pugh's Design Boundary Model shows 32 different facets of the business environment that can be taken into account during the development of the specification document. This model is used in this research to represent the basis of design thinking required to develop a product or service specification.

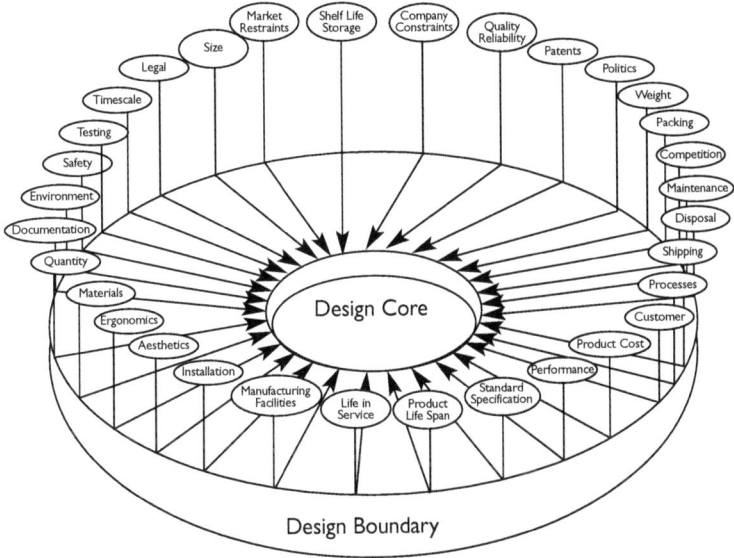

There are many areas where the public sector procurement function can benefit from using design thinking and design processes within the context of their role in procurement of goods and services and in the management of the supply chain. Many of these factors are implicitly considered in the evaluation of products offered from the market place. However, when they are made more explicit in the consideration of product or service need, there is an improvement in the end product or service choice. Generally speaking, knowledge of what influences product design, customer choice, the design processes and management issues pertinent to the acquisition of goods and services will serve to make more rounded professionals who will ultimately be better equipped to perform many tasks required of them in today's buying world.

Design impacts upon three fundamental issues: function, economics and aesthetics. Improved design effectiveness within the public sector could force down costs, ensure compliance with both legislation and standards, impact positively upon 'green procurement' and improve quality of life. To achieve design effectiveness there needs to be a recognition by buyers that more emphasis needs to be placed on the initial clarification of the user's requirements and the better capture and integration of those requirements. This would produce a more cohesive structured specification format compatible with the functionality of the design process that would then align product availability and user requirements. Design can therefore be used to better effect on both buyers' and sellers' sides of the market place.

The Design Council has been focusing, with dedicated research projects over the past years, on improving the use of design in the procurement of goods and services in the public sector. One of the main developments in this area was enhancing the professional procurement qualification programme with a more explicit understanding of design thinking. As a result the main programme – the Chartered Institute of Purchasing and Supply- Graduate Diploma has undergone major syllabus review to include design enhancements.

In addition the 'Best Practice Team' at the Chartered Institute has adopted the 'design concept' as an area within the procurement arena that needs further investigation. During such research projects, gaps were identified in the availability of suitable training materials to use within the cited education programmes for the purposes of demonstrating key factors such as:

- The importance of design thinking in procurement
- The need to involve many stakeholders at an early stage in the procurement process to ensure design incorporation and
- To permit dissemination of good design procurement processes

occurring within the public sector.

This book aims to begin to address these identified gaps by providing materials in the form of case studies and a study aid to specifically support the syllabus of the Chartered Institute of Purchasing and Supply Graduate Diploma programme amongst other procurement programmes available.

The case studies have been developed using a structured approach:

- Defining the aims of the public sector department or agency discussed
- Defining the aims and purpose of specific procurement, ie what was to be achieved in buying the specific procurement
- Examining how the specification or requirement documents were put together and the factors of design and procurement that were considered in its development
- Examining the process and interactions of relevant 'stakeholders' in the procurement process, ie purchasing, users, industry, engineers, designers, finance etc
- Explaining the outcome and level of success from the procurement, ie benefits and objectives achieved or issues that could be improved
- Identifying lessons learnt, ie why the procurement process was good or bad in its approach.

A set of clear objectives has been set for the investigation of the cases:

- A clear set of design parameters and boundaries
- A clear role for procurement within the organisation
- To cite the implications for incorrect purchases and the importance of the procurement to the organisation as a whole

- To focus on the technical/user interface in the identification and management of need established for the specific procurement
- To develop a perspective of the interface between the various stake holders using the following instances:

    Product/requirement definition

    Process operation and management

    Technical detail and complexity

    People factors

    Communication

    Organisation.

The organisations that have cooperated in the development of the case studies are as follows:

- Inland Revenue, England
- Belfast City Council, Northern Ireland
- Government Purchasing Agency, Northern Ireland
- Driving Test Standards Agency, England
- Driver and Vehicle Licensing Agency, S. Wales
- Local Authority, N. Ireland/England

Audiences and Uses of the Cases

The cases are suitable for final year and post-graduate students on a variety of courses including:

- Supply chain management
- Strategic purchasing
- Organisational behaviour
- General management, e.g. MBA.

Students need to be aware of the concepts of strategy, design concepts and public sector procedures before attempting the cases.

It is suggested that the lecturer divides the course members into groups of around five to six at most and they should then be asked to give a presentation on how they see the case scenario and how they would deal with specific questions and issues raised with each case.

Chapter 2
Inland Revenue Case Study

Introduction

This case study looks at the development of the furniture framework for Inland Revenue (IR) started in the 1980s and reviewed in 1999. The framework covered the procurement of:

- Desking and storage
- Seating
- Specialised storage
- Carpeting and floor cover.

The main focus for this work is on the desking and storage. In this furniture framework IR sought wider opportunities for Value For Money. They also saw this as an opportunity to enhance the staff working environment and morale in IR overall by showing the staff their value in considering new forms of office environments and working arrangements. IR too wished to be seen as a good employer who provides practical working environments and listens to its staff on what it needs to perform the many tasks asked off it. The plan was to also offer the staff the right to choose their own furniture and to design their working space that they hoped would add value to IR as a whole.

In the 1980s there was a high number of suppliers for this range of requirements. This was mainly due to the approach taken to procurement being decentralised to the various regional offices. There was in existence a traditional type furniture framework from which the regional offices could place orders on a local basis. The nature of furniture specified and the range of suppliers for it was diverse and plentiful.

It was decided by the IR procurement function that the entire furniture requirement could be managed more efficiently and effectively through some rationalisation of the choice of furniture currently available and the number of suppliers. As a result in 1983/84 the entire contract for furniture was re-tendered. Only six suppliers were selected from the evaluation process and a contract was let to them. This constituted a vast reduction on the previous approach to supplier numbers. Despite this reduction there were still issues of confusion on ordering and there were too many different specifications for IR to manage continuity of supply, and for a standardised office format to be developed.

By the mid-80s Inland Revenue had introduced a series of bespoke furniture, namely ION desks, to equip every tax office. The nature of the work in the tax offices meant that the standard office desk was too small to service the need for computers, tax files and other work too. This furniture was also still being manufactured in the 1983/84 period and this contract was running alongside the new furniture contract.

In the 1990s Inland Revenue made the decision to rationalise the entire furniture contract situation with a view to bringing the furniture and office layout for IR offices in line with each other and up to date.

The Inland Revenue offices had adopted an open plan approach to office layout system, but this was tempered with the need for private offices for the senior tax inspectors. This necessitated different desking from the bespoke desk. The contract for the manufacture of these desks was to run out in 1996. The existing framework too was to cease in 1996. By this time IR felt that its demand for the bespoke desking would be exhausted and the utilisation of offices had already begun to change significantly enough to review the entire requirement for furniture.

The Central Purchasing Unit of Inland Revenue decided in the early

1990s that it needed to place a central contract for all of the furniture needs, once the existing contracts expired at the end of 1996. There was a plan to learn for the development of the new contract from issues that had arisen on previous procurements.

Procurement Approach

As a result of an assessment of the situation Inland Revenue initially decided that the bespoke furniture was over-specified as it was made from metal componentry that had implications not only for usage but for housing and movement of the desks too. This had also a knock on effect to the space required for staff and the combination of furniture items needed to meet needs in local and regional offices. There had been some 22,000 of these bespoke desks initially purchased in the early 1980s. Some 10,000 were still in operation behind the enquiry counters in tax offices in the 1990s. The desks had initially proved successful in terms of space and usage, however there were major problems in terms of usage, portability and delivery difficulties that appeared to be consistent with over-engineering of the desks in the original specification.

A number of points was raised on the nature of furniture requirements, at this time, upon which IR could move forward:

- The bespoke desking ION was no longer needed.
- There was a reduced number of staff working in IR.
- There was to be a new office structure that fell out of the reduction of staff numbers. This would get rid of cellular offices and a re-structuring of local offices arranged. This would have significant impact on the needs identified for furniture for IR in the future.
- A background re-structure of offices revealed that where there were two offices in a reasonably sized town there should only now be one. This plan for re-structure was to be completed in phases and certain offices were reviewed against the new purpose for the offices.

Inland Revenue saw this re-structuring environment as an opportunity for not only the development of a central framework but also for a fresh initiative, especially since the bespoke desk requirements were coming to an end there was also a chance for new thinking. A process of wide consultation was embarked upon to move this initiative forward. Firstly it was decided to consult with industry to gain a feel for what furniture was available to IR, post 1996; this too would help to establish reliability in the products eventually offered and would ultimately meet with the expectation of the IR in going into such a framework. As a result an independent body called the Furniture Industrial Research Association (FIRA) was asked to make comment on the furniture needs of the IR. Trade Associations such as the Office Furniture Managers Association (OFMA) were approached too. IR had a dedicated space-planning unit based in Nottingham which had access to the latest technology such as Computer-Aided Design equipment used to plan and layout offices for the department. This group was approached to gain knowledge of how many offices existed and to provide plans of the new scale of space to be available after the re-structure for which they had developed a library of both office space and storage. It was decided then to consult with end users of furniture to ascertain their current feelings on the existing framework for furniture and the views and perceptions of all the staff on a proposed change to open plan offices, for instance.

The central procurement team led by HQ carried out an expenditure profile along with the types and usage of various existing ranges of furniture specified on the existing framework. From a design perspective IR were particularly interested in what made specific ranges more popular than others. As a result of the review IR were also able to make plans to refurbish offices and to sell off old furniture types in the process. The majority of the expenditure upon furniture lay with the regional offices so these offices were deemed good places to begin the consultation process. However, many of the offices seemed to be uncooperative or at best unhelpful in the provision of the information for a full assessment exercise. Not only did the IR central procurement staff find that the basis of the choice of ranges selected in the regional offices had much to do with the behaviour and popularity of the representative from the sales company but also that the choice was influenced by these representatives. The regional offices suspected the central procurement team from HQ as their main involvement up to that point had been to try to resolve issues between the user and the various suppliers of the products when problems arose. Another factor in the uncooperative nature of the staff at the regional offices was that they associated the changes in furniture and questions on their usage and choices of it to be somehow linked with the re-structure and so were distrustful of the change. The staff at these offices feared redundancies. There had been unbeknownst to the procurement team several leaks about major changes in IR. The procurement team had no prior knowledge of this and were advocating the need and desire for the closer involvement of the regional offices in the development of a bright new initiative to modernise the whole look of IR in terms of not only furniture but office layout too. Unfortunately the distrust evidenced itself in failure to divulge information to the procurement team. The staff appeared to be missing an opportunity to develop new office environments for themselves. This approach would take some work if meaningful data were to be collected.

Inland Revenue realised that as a result of environmental changes and new physical siting of staff that their annual expenditure on furniture was going to be much reduced on the previous year. They too had thoughts on seeking expertise outside of the main department and saw an opportunity to maintain the economies of scale previously attained on frameworks developed in the past by joining with another department. The Customs and Excise Department was asked to join in the project for a new look framework arrangement for furniture for the future. This decision led to discussions with Customs and Excise to discover any synergy between the two departments' requirements. A set of common items was established and general needs were identified. As a result both departments decided to continue with the project and establish a joint buying team made up of the IR central procurement unit and the Customs and Excise departmental purchasing agency. The departments felt that they needed to start work on the joint buying project some six to eight months prior to the release of the tender to the market place so as to gain as full a picture as possible of the needs of everyone concerned. This picture was to show the internal needs of the parties and the availability of the products in the market place too. It was agreed though that IR should be the main lead department for the project. Whilst the spend was dropping drastically within IR it was felt that Customs and Excise's requirements would keep up suppliers' interest in the framework and probably allow previously won discounts to be maintained. Much work ensued to determine the Customs and Excise background however; the agreement between them was to focus on common not specialised requirements for the department. Customs and Excise had areas within it to furnish which were rather unusual in their demands, such as the Ports and Dock areas. These were left out of the arrangement. Unfortunately Customs and Excise had neither the space-planning unit nor access to technology for the planning of it as IR had. This meant that they had to approach their data gathering and planning of requirement in a different way. They mostly talked to users to gain an idea of need and worked closely with the Customs and Excise Estates Unit to ascertain what was needed. As a result this department did not feel it necessary to consult the wider staff population, as they neither had a staff numbers reduction scheme not major re-structure to contend with at that time. This meant that the drivers for the joint arrangement were very different for the parties involved.

The project was well enough informed after the various consultations to proceed.

Specification of Needs

The next stage was to generate the specification with a more precise view of the current availability and approaches to office furnishing trends in the market. The new office environment needed to take account of new layout and usage for the working practices.

Some key information was put forward as the basis for the tender:

- There would be a need to reduce the number of suppliers again. Significant work had been completed on the earlier tender to do this but more could be done now. The joint procurement teams made a decision to appoint only four suppliers.

- The main criteria for the choice of both ranges and suppliers to supply them were to be based upon maintenance of choice to regional offices, to provide the regional offices with the ability to select what they wanted and the desire to maintain expenditure with fewer suppliers to sustain their interest in the venture. This mostly reflected the IR perspective.

- The framework had to be capable of offering a wide enough range of products and styles but to provide continuity as a generic standard across the departments. To this end the suppliers who were offered tenders could offer as many as six different ranges but they were told that not all might be acceptable on the framework in the final analysis.

- IR liked the size of the old bespoke desk but needed to take account of the need for cable management and flexibility of use. New office experiences were to lie in team working so whatever was to be offered would need to lend itself to team functioning within the environment. The new office environmental approach still however needed to take account of entitlements that certain grades gave individual staff members.

- Historically the IR desk and file storage system was communally based:

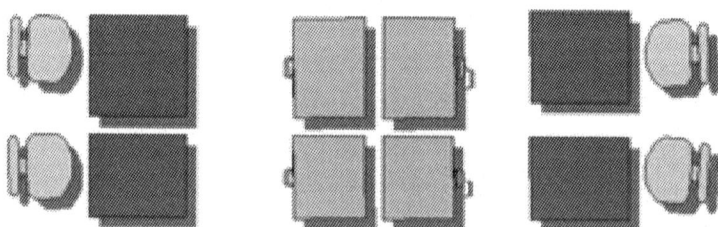

- The new plan for desking and storage proposed within the new framework would be one where staff had easier access to their own working papers and files. The storage needed to be aesthetically linked to each desk. The new approach would have to take account of the ergonomic issues pertinent to the use of equipment such as personal computers, etc.

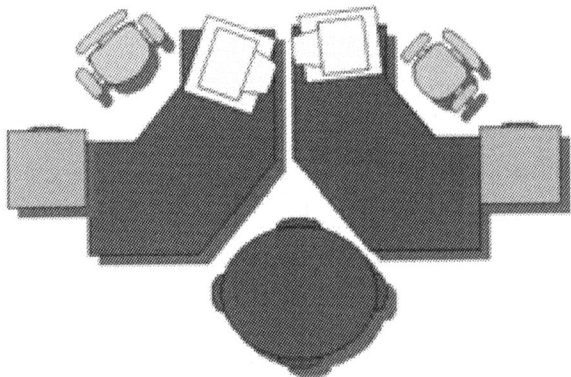

- Traditionally IR had only offered a narrow range of colours and woods in the range of furniture available to staff. This resulted in staff being forced to accept dictated furniture styles. The idea within the new framework was to make available many more options in terms of colour, wood, style and dimension so that staff could design furniture schemes for their own offices. The fact that open plan offices was to be the dominant approach to layout meant that staff had much more scope to design their own schemes, as they liked. In the choice of ranges offered by suppliers there would be sufficient scope for not only designing an attractive office scheme but to take account of grade and utilisation needs too.
- Attention was paid to legal elements of the specification. For instance where the furniture was being supplied though manufactured elsewhere there needed to be an understanding that any patents held on manufacture were legal and that the seller had the right to sell the goods which is deemed to be implicit in the sale agreement.

- It was decided by the central procurement team in IR that light oak was to be a base standard option offered on the framework and other woods and finishes were to be available for staff to select. There was of course a need for regional offices for example to be cost conscious and this was to be made clear before the start of the use of the framework. To this end staff needed to base their choice on what they could afford from an annual budget allocated for furniture.

- IR had to recognise certain constraints in the development of both the requirements and the framework itself. Cost was of course one, as mentioned above. The ethos of the departments too had to be taken into account, i.e. activity and usage versus free choice of items. There was recognition that all furniture could not be replaced with new furniture so the changes needed to be both gradual and fitting. Competition law that very much dictated the process for the framework development binds both departments.

- The tender then encouraged suppliers to offer as many varieties of furniture as they wished and no restrictions were to be placed upon them save that of the need for light oak desking as a base line. Cost and ethos considerations as givens, IR wished the choice to be as free as possible to the staff in terms of design and in fact wished the furniture offered to be of the sort that was made available within the private sector offices. This would also help to reflect the modern approach that departments such as IR and Customs and Excise were taking to their 'business affairs'.

The Procurement Procedure

A fully constituted tender board was set up consisting of two members from the Central Procurement Unit of IR, two representatives from Customs and Excise in the form of a departmental purchasing officer and a person from their Estates Department. There was also one representative from the Space Planning Unit from IR. Much information had now been collated from various sources through the consultation process that could now be used to formulate the tender document. It was decided at this stage by the board not to pass on data that had been made available on modern office layout and environments, from FIRA and the trade associations to the staff in general around IR. This decision was based on knowledge of strong personalities particularly within the regional offices who might have the ability to distort what was offered as information to consider new approaches to office design. However there were issues such as departmental constraints on the public purse, the culture of the working environment and the need to consider the purpose for the offices as part of the mission for IR and indeed this applied to Customs and Excise too. It was then the plan to try to stabilise focus on the furniture and office design within IR and Customs and Excise rather than to provide the opportunity for staff to visualise extremes in their choice of design that they might see in the industry data. The tender board all agreed that it was critical to seize this new opportunity to offer modern office design systems within the framework that the staff at IR and Customs and Excise could select for themselves. The new framework though as it transpired was not as marked a change from the previous one when compared to the distinctive changes that had been introduced with the bespoke desking in mid-1980 or after its demise in the 1990s.

It was hoped that the new framework would signal a more modern approach to furniture in general and that it would be acceptable to all staff as a better option for them than the previous framework. The creation of a new departmental environment was at stake in this framework where freer choices could be offered in open plan offices. The devolvement of budgets too helped to provide a more positive relationship between central procurement and the users within the departments.

Inland Revenue provided a reflection on the new approach that they were taking to the furniture framework. They felt that it was functional, very practical in its form and would be more aesthetically pleasing to staff at the same time. There had not been an explicit mention of the recognised link between working environment and the productivity of staff within the working environment. There was still however the recognition that the new framework, to be successful, needed to be adopted throughout the IR. There was still potential for failure with this new approach because there remained fear of the unknown re-structure and axing of staff numbers and positions. There was a common belief still held by many staff members within IR that if new furniture was offered jobs and people would go. This, unless clarified, had the potential to overshadow the opportunity to develop a new working environment.

By the time the tender was to be despatched potential suppliers in the market were eagerly awaiting the opportunity to bid for the contract/framework. Much news had filtered into this market as a result of frequent visits to suppliers and as the result of the specific development of knowledge of current trends available to buyers at this time. There was a conscious decision not to formally involve the industry or wider market place in the development of the requirement in the early process for several reasons. Firstly it was intended that the full requirement would be put to competitive bidding and early involvement of suppliers might prejudice that competitive bidding process. Secondly, the joint tender board wished to maintain an open mind on what was available from different sources of supply; they feared that working more closely with suppliers in the early stages might have clouded that view or distorted the picture of what was available to them. Sufficient information could be gathered, it was felt, from the market and through the advice of the IR Space Planning Unit to determine what was required and to allow the market to respond to those requirements. It was therefore a conscious decision to approach individual suppliers to seek information and collect brochures to complete their initial research. Due to time and the fact that IR had a larger requirement than Customs and Excise, it was decided that the initial data gathering would be done solely by the IR representatives and then passed on to Customs and Excise for their consideration. Unfortunately this approach caused some difficulties for the development of the joint requirement, as IR could not find compatibility amongst the breadth of Customs and Excise needs; it proved difficult to find common areas of need. Despite this there was a belief that commonality of suppliers between both departments made total sense.

Nevertheless, the market was becoming excited at the prospect of new styles and designs being considered by what might be perceived to be a regular public sector department with the staid image that that conjured up. It was not at that time recognised by the furniture market that the expenditure on furniture for the joint tender might be less than the individual requirements expenditure for IR alone. In the 1996/7 financial expenditure year some 4.5 million pounds was spent and whilst this had peaked at 6 million pounds the overall expenditure was dramatically falling to represent more in the region of 1.5 million pounds.

Inland Revenue's tender board's initial fact-finding had revealed that the market could offer them what was needed so competition for the requirements was the next step. The IR and Customs and Excise departments, indeed all public sector entities within the EU, are subject to the Public Sector Procurement Directives which quite clearly lay down the parameters for procurement in the market arena. Fair competition rules apply to the majority of purchases and specific timescales also apply in the advertisement and operation of the tender process.

Inland Revenue suggested an innovative approach to try to include staff wishes in the selection of the furniture for the framework. They decided to set out a demonstration of a sample of the ranges offered by the tendered suppliers at their Nottingham Space Planning Unit premises. As there was to be a fixed time and space for the event potential suppliers were to deliver a mock-up office layout for a generic workstation accompanied by other furniture which matched in for inspection by staff who would be invited to view it. All staff were given the opportunity to travel to Nottingham to see the furniture offered and to make comment upon it through specifically designed sheets left beside the ranges for their use. The demonstration remained in place for two weeks. Staff could either fill in the comment sheets at the time or return them in letterform within a designated period.

The culmination of six to eight months' research set IR and Customs and Excise in a position to issue an advertisement through Europe for their complete requirement. There were 70 expressions of interest in the framework mostly from the UK but also from Scandinavia, Germany,

France and Italy. The tender board reduced the expressions of interest to only ten companies who were despatched tenders in accordance with the restricted procedures of the EU Procurement Directives applicable to the procurement of goods within the public sector. The breakdown of country of origin of these ten saw eight UK firms, an Italian and a Swedish company. The companies had to be financially sound and were asked to supply financial data to inform the tender board of their particular standing in this regard. There was also a questionnaire issued to the ten companies to establish their technical capacity, such as quality standards, etc. Only seven firms responded out of the ten who were sent tender documents. On investigation as to why three had not returned the tender IR were able to establish that the reasons found related to the onerous nature of the specification or the fact that companies had decided to merge thus reducing the number of suppliers in the market place. Companies who returned tender documents were invited to submit the planned demonstration pieces and the technical capacity questionnaire was assessed through the allocation of scores on preset criteria such as ergonomics, quality and durability. IR had taken advice from experts at the furniture buyers forum in respect of any problem areas experienced previously and particular desires in respect of ease of use, etc. The Ministry of Agriculture Fisheries and Foods had also produced a report of standards for furniture that had helped in the development of the specification in respect of weights and heights for 'safe' working conditions.

The demonstration phase of the tender worked well to both offer suppliers a fair chance to have their wares considered and to include staff in the choice and preferences for furniture to be placed upon the framework. There was a fair degree of commonality between the ranges offered however this was to some degree expected as the market for furniture is plentiful and of course to meet the tender specification offers from suppliers would be in the same standard range and style requirements.

Inland Revenue had learned valuable lessons from the development of the bespoke furniture in terms of the lack of flexibility and longevity of service of the desks. This time there was a stipulation placed upon suppliers that those ranges that were offered had to be available to IR and Customs and Excise for at least ten years however the suppliers could enter new ranges as older ranges were withdrawn from the general market place. To this end the stipulation was that the furniture was expected to have a minimum life of ten years in service. Whilst ten years was to be the expected life of the furniture, lessons had been learned from the bespoke furniture contract that a tie-in to a particular supplier(s) for ten years was far too long. It was agreed by the tender board that a period of three years with the potential to extend the contract a year at a time up to a total of five years was appropriate. There were also thoughts in IR at this time of future approaches to working in offices and the concept of 'hot desking' was mooted. This concept offers no individual a set working position but sets out a series of desks which any individual can utilise by tapping into phone lines and pc's to operate for a period of time. Today's working environment necessitates attendance at many meetings, some overseas, and permits staff to work from their homes through the use of IT, so there will not be as many staff working on any one day in office conditions as in previous years. A period of contract that remained constant for longer than five years might, it was felt, restrict IR and Customs and Excise freedom to move to more modern approaches to working in the new millennium.

Significant added value was achieved on the framework too as suppliers offered a 'free' space planning and utilisation service to all offices who ordered furniture from them.

The result of the tender exercise was that a contract was awarded in line with the ethos of IR and Customs and Excise departments. It was believed to be good practice by the central procurement team. It also fitted in with the values and plans for IR in the future in terms of open plan office environments for instance. The contract/framework was awarded to only four suppliers, but solely for desking. The tender board considered awarding to only three suppliers but decided that this was probably insufficient to cope and would reflect a more dramatic drop in suppliers for the framework. The seating requirements were compiled as a separate framework and research was undertaken to match desks and seating for a later date once the existing seating framework expired. It was decided that the continuation of the joint tender process between IR and Customs and Excise should be maintained for this. The completion of the EU tendering procedure required that a contract award notice be placed in the Official Journal of the European Communities (OJEC).

Contract Management

The nature of the framework was such that it was not mandatory in its use throughout the departments. However, the actual take up was calculated as around 85%. This was deemed to be because the staff had been fully informed of what was being done on furniture buying within the departments and the fact that staff were encouraged to be fully involved in the practice of selection, etc.

The contract commenced on 1st January 1998 and was divided between two UK companies, a Swedish company and an Italian company. All companies had offices in the UK.

As IR and Customs and Excise knew of the two UK companies awarded the framework previously it was hard to get the staff to accept the foreign suppliers furniture at the start, particularly the Italian ranges. Despite the choice being given to staff prior to contract award it was felt that old habits die hard amongst the IR staff and so continuance to work with more traditional designs remained the norm for a period of time of some four months. Slowly though the orders began to be placed across the four furniture suppliers to the effect that the take up was eventually evenly spread across them. The Swedish company made a review of the market and of the IR/Customs and Excise contract and explained that they would go through a re-structure for their company in the wider market place which meant that they were not now as interested in the business of this particular contract.

Inland Revenue completed a series of reviews one initially after the framework was let and then a fuller review of the furniture after one year.

At first there were moans and groans expressed by either phone calls or letters about the furniture and the suppliers. Staff expressed their scepticism of so few suppliers being able to satisfy them. The later review however, found the framework was deemed a success as there was now a 90% take up of the items identified on the framework. The general consensus was that it met the needs of the staff in terms of the style and ranges offered and that many staff were pleasantly surprised by the choice and their ability to make it within cost conscious parameters set by their budgets. It not only was serviceable and durable but looked good too. A common comment from feedback received was that the furniture was aesthetically pleasing. The contract is due to expire on its three-year date at the beginning of 2001.

Conclusions

This contract was offered up a model contract in respect of the ability to research the requirements both inside and outside the departments concerned. There was too a desire to incorporate design features and current trends for not only furnishing but also the entire office environment management process. Factors such as quality, Health & Safety and ergonomics were explicitly considered within the development of the framework. The process also included interfaces within the department to encourage staff to own the furniture framework and to take pride in how their offices looked and operated. A heavy emphasis was placed upon work with industry and furniture buying experts to ensure a firm idea of what was required from usability aspects as well as durability aspects. Performance of the furniture and the supplier of it was key in ensuring that the staff using the framework remained happy. To this end standards and measures had been entered into the specification to ensure quality, delivery and specified lead times from the placement of the order to the delivery to the customer. A sophisticated pricing scheme was devised to manage the cost structure for IR/Customs and Excise and for suppliers too. There was a firm price agreed for a period of one year subject to increases capped by statistics from the Office of National Statistics based upon Retail Price Index.

The price of the product was of course only a factor in the costing of the entire framework that was deemed more relevant. To this end each supplier needed to provide a price index containing details of the wood and metal componentary and the pricing structure for that. IR devised formula proportions to help calculate what would be a fair price for the items offered. It was practically very hard to deal with.

Disposal of old furniture items was now a consideration that had to be built in to contracts with the pressure on environmentally friendly processes in government. IR had tried many ways and times to execute the disposal of furniture it seemed to no avail. The fact that the desking had been set in IR as having a ten-year life made disposal more difficult as it was worth very little. Whilst the tender for the current framework had explored the disposal issue with the suppliers there was no take up of this point on the eventual framework. When the IR central procurement team visited the cites of offices using the new furniture there was an increasing amount of questions on disposal of furniture from a wide variety of offices throughout the UK. It was decided to advertise that IR had surplus furniture which proved effective to the extent that the Valuation Agency took some off IR's hands to replace their own.

A strong element of the success of the framework lay in the fact that there was a maintenance agreement to back up the supply. When an issue rose the supplier would first be invited to visit the office to inspect the furniture and its condition. A condition of repair or replacement was operated based upon the attribution of blame in the incident, however IR had been working hard to establish good relationships with the suppliers so it was felt that the parties would not come to blows over this.

Lessons Learnt

- The procurement team was asked to consider the contractual approach and the inclusion of the cited design criteria after the completion of the contract. They identified these lessons:

  IR felt that extra effort put in at the start to research, develop and discuss the requirements for both departments paid off, in many ways:

  Sound specification of need

  Understanding of how the market operated

  Awareness of what the market could offer

  The current climate of unease within IR and how this affected contracting for furniture

  The benefits of internal interfacing with customers

  The smooth operation of the framework throughout the two departments.

  IR realised the importance of the inclusion of design factors into the development of the specification and the effect of this on the success of the entire framework.

- When IR undertook the expenditure profiles for furniture at the regional offices they found that insufficient thought was being put into the procurement of furniture. Users were not considering what the furniture was designed to be used for prior to purchase. Desking was being used mainly as filing areas or for the storage of files. They felt that there was a lack of expertise in procurement that needed to be remedied through support and education from the central procurement team. This would have the knock-on effect of removing waste and reducing costs throughout the department.

- The pricing structure and formula designed for the contract was too onerous for all concerned. It took time and resources to calculate. This needed to be rectified for future framework design.

- There was a localised fear of representatives from furniture companies entering IR offices due to past experience of 'hard sell' tactics and this resulted in many offices not taking full advantage of the 'free office planning' facility that had been negotiated into the framework. To remedy this and to provide a full knowledge platform from which staff could use the framework a 'Best Buyers Guide' was developed by the central procurement team to explain what exactly is on the framework. This guide was created in an A4 ring binder, laid out supplier by supplier, setting out all costs, designs, linedrawings and plans, photographs, lead times, ordering details and contract details. Each supplier was encouraged to provide colour charts of design and ranges including pricing, etc to submit within the guide. This of course needed to be kept up to date.

- IR had decided to keep on short term a contract with the bespoke desking developed solely for IR. This was held as a sort of comfort blanket to IR. This was not required as no one requested these desks at all. There was some concern in this regard about throwing out the old and bringing in the new. The IR culture was strong and the IR central procurement team felt that there was a likelihood this culture would prevail despite the new moves to change it. Their fears were largely unfounded as staff after a slow start actually embraced the new styles and any initial mistrust of quality, value for money, and fitness for purpose in respect of weights and heights, etc were diminished by the strength of the framework and the relationship with the suppliers. The norm is now that the regional offices notify all the suppliers of their requirements and discuss them in respect of the people involved and the ranges available within cost parameters. They have even had the opportunity to set up a 'beauty parade' of furniture from various suppliers for staff to examine. The cost and style factor discounts can be taken into account and the majority decision chooses the office furniture.

- The issue of disposal has become quite a problem as a result of the failure to deal with this effectively. The issue has increased in priority as the take up of procurement of new furniture increases too.

- The framework became so successful that a mandatory status was not required. However, the latest print of the best buyers guide included a clause that said that the regional offices can buy their furniture requirements from sources outside the framework. However, sound reasons for doing so would be expected to accompany any external orders, specifically mentioning reasons why the official framework was not utilised.

Case Synopsis

This true case describes the generation of a 'new look' furniture framework contract currently used within the Inland Revenue (IR) and the Customs and Excise departments of the UK central government. The departments seized the opportunity to fully consider the furniture requirements in light of organisational changes and more modern working patterns operating in the public and private sectors, such as team meetings and home working. In this furniture framework IR sought wider opportunities for Value for Money. They too saw this as an opportunity to enhance the staff working environment and morale in IR overall showing the staff their value in considering new forms of office environments and working arrangements. IR too wished to be seen as a good employer who provides practical working environments and one that listens to its staff on what is needed to perform the many tasks asked of it. The plan was to also offer the staff the right to choose their own furniture and to design their working space that they hoped would add value to IR as a whole. The approach that was taken to the development of the contract to back up their furniture requirements was innovative and IR sought to learn from past 'mistakes' by seeking to embark on a strategic procurement path and to explicitly include design concepts and criteria in the framework and specification design. They too wished to exploit external and internal expertise and experience in the development of this framework document. This approach shows a model strategic procurement approach:

- Planning ahead
- Incorporating a broad understanding of organisation, market and product criteria in the development of the framework document
- Learning from the past
- Considering stakeholders' views
- Working with suppliers and industry
- Adding value to the process by working on cost not just price.

In addition the strengths of the work and the success factors for this project have been attributed to the broad consideration of design issues early on in the development process and by reviewing the work done to ensure effective best practice in procurement in the future.

Teaching and Learning Objectives

- To provide students with the opportunity to understand a case relaying best practice in the public sector procurement arena that explicitly incorporates design concepts early in its procurement strategy.
- To help students understand areas of synergy between design criteria for the development of new products and the procurement criteria for the development of sound procurement decisions.
- To provide scope to analyse the design issues considered in the development of a furniture framework.
- To examine the effect of design on procurement strategies.
- To explore the importance of involving key stakeholders in the procurement process throughout.

Main Issues Raised

- Consideration of design concepts
- Consideration of the impact of design upon the identification of need
- Consideration of design upon the finished procurement contract
- Consideration of procurement decision criteria
- Consideration of the value of procurement research
- Consideration of key elements of strategic procurement
- Consideration of the importance of external and internal interface in the development of the requirement for procurement
- Consideration of the impact of organisational values, mission and culture upon procurement decisions
- Consideration of supplier/buyer relationships
- Consideration of EC Procurement Directives
- Consideration of issues such as Intellectual Property Rights and legal factors in the develpment of procurement contract.

Specific Questions

1. Consider the IR case study in the light of the Pugh Model of Design Boundaries provided in the introduction to this book, to determine how and in what depth the cited 'design' and 'procurement' were considered in the development of this furniture framework.

2. Consider how important the inclusion of these criteria is to the success of the entire project.

3. Identify the involvement of the various stakeholders in this case study process and explain the role that they played in the development of the final framework.

4. Draw a flow diagram to show the stages of involvement of these stakeholders through the development of the framework process.

The Approach Taken

The case has been written with full cooperation of the Inland Revenue's Central Procurement Team. The case was approached from the perspective of design issues and how they had or had not been incorporated into the procurement strategy of the IR. The full approach in terms of questioning and method has been incorporated into the chapter of introduction in this text. The Pugh Model of Design Boundaries has been used to identify the main elements considered in new product design and those most pertinent to criteria for making decisions for various procurements throughout both the private and public sectors. This model was identified at the end of the interview with a representative of the IR's Central Procurement Team.

Question 1 - Guide to Inclusion of Design boundary criteria - as identified in the colour adapted model of Pugh 1991.

- Central Procurement team IR
- Departmental Procurement Team - Customs and Excise
- Estate Unit Customs and Excise
- Space Planning Unit - IR
- Industry - FIRA
- Trade Associations - OFMA
- Furniture Suppliers
- Regional Office Staff
- Valuation Agency

Chapter 3
Belfast City Council Case Study - Café at the Crematorium

Introduction

This case study examines the plans to develop a waiting area with some basic café facilities at the crematorium in Belfast, Northern Ireland. It explains the process to develop the design and the contract approach to the extension project for the work on an existing site. It is design rich and has highlighted some interesting issues not only in determining and understanding the vagaries of establishing the requirement for a potentially emotive area, surrounding many beliefs and rituals, death and dignity, but, also the process of contract development.

The contract itself has arisen from a perceived need to provide facilities for the bereaved attending cremation services and those visiting the graves of loved ones. The position of the crematorium in Belfast is not remote however there was no facility for people to obtain even tea or coffee. Many people would travel long distances to attend funerals and no facilities existed for them so the Belfast City Council sought to address this need.

The Belfast City Council is the largest of 26 Councils in Northern Ireland and has 51 elected members. The council serves a population of 297,100 and manages an annual expenditure of £ 63. 5million, operating from 101 locations and employing around 2,493 people.

Belfast City Council's aim is to provide effective civic leadership for the people of Belfast by providing beneficial services to local communities and by representing their best interests in consultation with other public services. The City Council will work to ensure that Belfast, the major city of Northern Ireland, becomes safe, attractive, healthy, environmentally sustainable and economically viable and that the Council itself earns a reputation of fairness and efficiency.

(Belfast City Council 1997).

The project itself was mooted some two years previous to the commencement of the development work upon it. The City Council wished to provide sustainable development that would enhance the existing environment. They sought to improve services for the public. However, due to a Council re-organisation, the work had not been progressed. However, there was sufficient political pressure in 1999 to promote the development of the project. It was envisaged that the budget for the work would be around £300,000 which would include construction and consultation fees. The entire process would be a long one in which approvals, scheme design, detailed design and a competitive tender exercise would be undertaken. The project development work would begin in May 2000 with a minimum start date for completion of the work laid out as April 2001.

Background to the Case

Only one crematorium exists in Northern Ireland; it is situated on the site of the City Cemetery on the outskirts of Belfast, the capital. Anyone in Northern Ireland wishing to use the crematorium must therefore travel to the city. The crematorium was built some 40 to 50 years ago. As a nation the Northern Irish population, in the past, favoured traditional burial services to the more modern approach of cremation. However, the City Council noted an increase in requests for cremation services from 2400 to

2700 in one year. The crematorium had in the past been open for business between the hours of 9.30am and 3.30pm. The increase in workload meant that the crematorium needed to be opened longer to cope, as it had to provide more service time for the numbers required. The new hours of business from 1999 then became 8.30am to 4.30pm. A set time was allocated to the provision of the each funeral service of around 40 minutes. No cremation services were held on a Sunday. The crematorium is subject to environmental protection legislation concerning the levels of emission from the crematorium. The City Council was aware that the standards of the crematorium in Northern Ireland do not meet those on the mainland. There would be a cost of £500million to bring the crematorium up to the requirements. This cost included an allocation for more facilities to cope with the cited increase in trends for more cremations. There was a suggestion that the crematorium should be relocated to a new site as 60 to 70 percent of the burials in the country were requested from the Belfast population. This meant that the rise in the numbers of cremations was coming from outside the city boundaries. Another alternative was to request monies from the other local councils to support the costs of running the crematorium in Belfast. These matters would take time to resolve.

The crematorium was laid out in such a way that mourners arrived with the hearse. All entered the building along a corridor into the chapel, through one dedicated doorway at the front of the building. The service was conducted and the coffin was removed from the chapel underground to be cremated. Once the service was over the mourners were ushered out through a door at the side of the chapel into a passageway that now contained the mourners' wreathes and floral tributes. This gave the mourners a further opportunity to express their condolences to close family members before all participants had to leave the building through a door at the end of that passage leading to the side of the building. As one family moved through into the chapel through the main entrance, another family would have just left the chapel and was congregating in the passageway after their service. This chain of events occurred throughout the day as each service was concluded and a new one was began. At no time did one family meet another, so that each service was conducted for that family and no other could intrude upon their grief. The building design and later developments facilitated this in the form of a series of corridors towards the outer walls of the building. The cremation took place in the undercroft of the building. The internal area of the building was laid out as a courtyard. This area had not previously been opened to the public but it was visible as a pleasant garden for those passing through the building.

One gap in the service provision discovered by staff working there was that there was nowhere that families, who may have travelled a considerable distance, could obtain even basic refreshments at such a difficult time. Consultants were asked to identify areas within the existing design that could house such a facility. The courtyard area at the centre of the building was suggested for the purpose.

Much work needed to go into the planning of this facility prior to its development as many factors had to be considered. The level of disruption that might be caused whilst building work was undertaken also had to be considered, as this was the only facility in the country and no delay or cremation postponement was acceptable.

Factors for Consideration in the Development of the Requirement

The City Council employed consultants to undertake research into the possibility of providing a waiting area within which some catering facilities could be provided for mourners. A survey of those using the crematorium facilities was undertaken to determine if the City Council's perception of a need for café facilities reflected the desires of the public and, if so, what form they should take. The consultative process that began in June 2000 involved interviews with mourners and staff working at the facility. Those businesses that had direct links with the crematorium such as funeral directors, florists, and clergy of various faiths, etc were also involved in the research process, as their business would be directly affected either positively or negatively by the intended changes. The consultant sought to learn what the mourners thought of the facilities as they then stood, and how they might like them improved. They invited any ideas to improve the service overall as an experience for those using the crematorium. The research population upon which to conduct the research was hard to define. Would the most appropriate people to interview be those who had just used the facility, those who had recently used facility or those likely in the future to use the facility. Given that people rarely like to discuss death or anything to do with it in advance of meeting the actual situation, the wider population proved to be difficult to obtain a response from. It was decided to interview those using the facility and those who recently used the facility. The interviews themselves had to be done in a sensitive manner as mourners leaving the crematorium might not be prepared to answer questions about the facilities or indeed their experience might be influenced by the way the service had been handled by any individual in contact with the process or by their own level of grief.

The entire business of death and funerals is emotive and needs to be handled sensitively. Religious and cultural norms strongly influence the form of funeral rites. Some people will have left instructions on how their funeral and affairs are to be conducted. There is then a heavy onus upon their next of kin not only to organise the funeral day respectfully but also to be seen to do so. Thus, many of the people who might use the crematorium whether representing businesses or not, have specific views and stances on what should or should not be included in the facilities there. This naturally affected the acceptability of the services offered by the City Council at the crematorium.

The City Council was not only constrained by the demands of the public that they served, but also by the nature of this type of business. Funerals are inevitably emotionally charged, and what would be a minor inconvenience in another situation could prove to be the catalyst for exaggerated response. As more and more cremations were required from the only crematorium in the country, pressure on the facilities, and on the level of service that could be offered was increased. The City Council had already extended the working day, to try to meet this increasing demand for the services and, hand in hand with this, strove to ensure timely utilisation of the facilities. That is, the City Council was required to manage the flow of business effectively.

The City Council and its staff were keen to try to minimise distress to mourners, by offering a friendly, respectful, and appropriate quality of service. Delay to any part of the proceedings would potentially be distressing for the mourners; such stress in an emotionally charged context could have longer lasting effects if mourners perceived that they had failed to meet their obligations toward the recently deceased, through such delays. There would also be a multiplier effect on the work of the funeral directors, florists, clergy and indeed the crematorium staff, who are all too conscious of the need to provide a consistently high level of service for all their customers. Of course, these staff are also bound to react at a human level.

The emphasis for the crematorium is one of customer focus. The sensitivities of the business require the provision of a service that meets public need. Whilst there are clear market and company constraints upon the business at the crematorium that would suggest that the development of this contract would add difficulties to the overall performance of the crematorium, the City Council endeavoured to provide some level of service for the public. It is the main purpose of this contract and the design criteria surrounding the development of the waiting area with catering facilities to provide a new service for mourners (customers) using the crematorium.

The City Council, therefore, discovered counter demands upon the utilisation of the facilities that affected the plans for the new waiting area. On one hand, the funeral experience in its form had to demonstrate a stately respect for those involved. For mourners, the business of the crematorium was secondary to their purpose at the facility. Many mourners find the entire process upsetting. While dealing with their own grief and their obligations to the deceased they are gathering together with family and friends whom they might not have seen for years. They need and want time to meet, to reflect and to deal with this situation. On the other hand those involved on a practical level at the crematorium are anxious to ensure a good level of service to each group of mourners, throughout each day. However, one criterion for achieving the desired performance of the facility, for all concerned, is the timely management of each event. Of necessity they have to be concerned with the throughput of business, and this depends upon the pacing of each event. They are concerned, at the very least, with the flow of the entire process, not only in terms of the length of service but also the arrival times of hearses, mourners, flowers, etc and indeed, equally, with their departures from the various areas of the building. Unless these are carefully managed and the required numbers of cremations take place, serious problems might arise. Delays of funerals, overlapping of funeral parties, etc would increase distress as well as attracting adverse publicity for the City Council and associated businesses.

Specific Consideration for the Waiting Area

The consultant's research revealed that there was indeed a requirement for some indoor waiting facility that provided catering. As a minimum, the requirement for any waiting area with catering facilities had to maintain a balance between the identified two counter approaches; this was to prove hard to achieve. Some issues that were highlighted as important in the consideration of the design of the waiting area included the need to maintain a dignified atmosphere while meeting the individual needs of multiple groups of mourners and allowing the normal progress of work within the crematorium. There would need to be an understanding that people might appreciate an area where they could wait and enjoy some light catering facilities without encouraging them to settle for any length of time, as this would jeopardise the entire business of the day.

Many members of the public interviewed, commented that they had found the crematorium building to be situated in an exposed part of the cemetery and therefore the Northern Irish climate that threw up cold, rain and wind at regular intervals was a further unwelcome condition along with their grief. The mourners felt also that they would like the opportunity to meet with family and friends after the service as well as seeking shelter and the opportunity to meet family and friends beforehand. A tradition in this country was to hold a 'wake' for the deceased where all the mourners gathered for food and drink in memory of their loved one after the funeral service was over. This event normally took place in the home of the deceased or of a member of their family. Some of the mourners who were interviewed stated that many of their group had travelled long distances and lived in different parts of the country. They felt that a room for a wake at the crematorium would have been convenient. However, access to the waiting area had to be controlled and managed by staff at the crematorium, to ensure the quality of service to all as discussed already. It was felt that there was not the room to provide such an area and that such facilities were outside of the remit of responsibility of the City Council. Similarly, the request for alcohol to be served as part of such catering facilities was deemed inappropriate.

The City Council therefore limited the primary purpose of the waiting area to an indoor meeting place for mourners to use prior to the chapel service. This necessitated specific entry and exit restrictions to the waiting room as only those mourners waiting to attend the next funeral service would be permitted entry and they had to be ushered out of the room in time for the appropriate funeral service into the chapel. There could only be one route in to the area and one route out. The positioning of doors then became a more specific focus for architects.

The management of groups of mourners too would become a greater responsibility for staff as they felt it important that any plans should include opportunities to separate different families, so as to provide privacy while maintaining reverence in the main service area. A waiting area that could be partitioned to allow different family mourning groups to be accommodated in the area but to do so separately might be appropriate so as to ease tension and permit shared grief to be expressed. Ushers on duty at the entrance would be required which would add to the staffing requirements at the crematorium.

However, noise created in this area, especially if it was to include a café, and that of the people using it, as well as the machinery within the site, had to be managed. Acoustics was therefore an important aspect as no one wanted funeral services to be disrupted by the chatting and reminiscing of other groups of mourners, nor indeed for such chatter to be drowned out by the mechanical sounds of a working crematorium. Likewise, due to the necessity to meet time pressure on the services, it was felt by crematorium staff and designers that there should be no seating for mourners in the waiting area that might encourage them to settle into noisy chatter rather than moving on to other events of the day. As the waiting area required space for more than one family group, and the requirement for separation of these families from each other, seating was deemed to take up too much valuable space.

The crematorium staff had identified behavioural traits of those attending services at the crematorium. Emotions ran high at time of bereavement and therefore people could be unpredictable in how they expressed their grief. A wide range of reactions had surfaced during events at the crematorium spanning from crying to fighting and hysteria, as members of families that perhaps had not met up for years reunited, fell into disagreement or reacted to others' emotional outburst, despite their meeting being for the purpose of a funeral. For this reason and those discussed surrounding emotional outbursts, the suggestion for partitioning to divide off areas of the café from each other and to help diffuse any sound that might travel was reinforced.

Factors such as the selection of colour schemes and types of music that might be played in the waiting area were important considerations. Some colours were deemed more appropriate than others; people's reactions to colour scheme choice could affect their mood. Similarly, the traditions surrounding the funeral rite meant that colours such as black or dark colours would be seen as more appropriate than bright colours in most circumstances. This would also be the case in the form of music played. Moods might be lifted or dropped through the music piped in the background of the waiting area. Strong views were held on the kind of music, if any, that might be played in such an area.

Another key consideration was the type of catering facilities to offer at the crematorium. Alcoholic beverages had been ruled out but it was not clear as to what catering to offer mourners, whether only beverages such as tea or coffee should be made available or whether to include food. The scale of food preparation required would affect the size of the area, equipment and staffing requirement needed. The time available to serve food and drink to those awaiting the start of the next service was limited and thus would limit the range of what catering could be offered. As there were to be no seats in the area, there could be no tables but it was difficult to envisage how people would manage to hold perhaps a cup and plate and dispose of such food and drink receptacles without some surface to place them on. So the intended layout for the waiting area would limit the service provision also. Similarly, food and drink preparation naturally causes aroma. There needed to be great care taken in terms of how any smell that was created by the café was managed for fear of its escape outside the area perhaps into the chapel. It would not be acceptable for the aroma of coffee or that of a pie or pasty to waft out of the waiting area even into the passageway. To contain the unwanted aroma, either inside or outside the area, would require attention to again the positioning of the doors and also the ventilation and filters to defuse aromas.

The entire appearance and layout of the waiting area had to be in keeping with the environmental circumstances and also has to facilitate a specific ambience. Staff working within the crematorium in general work in an emotionally charged environment. Those responsible for serving within the described waiting area would find themselves in close proximity with mourners. Given the circumstances of the business of the crematorium these particular staff will perhaps stay longer in contact with these mourners than any of the others working in the building. The training that would be required for the staff to be able to deal with people under these circumstances needed to be considered too.

The Contract Process

The contract process began in May 2000 when some quotations for consultative developmental work were issued. These were returned in June. The procurement team at the City Council undertook an analysis of quality and price considerations and appointed a consultant at the end of the same month. The consultant was required, from 28 July, to develop a scheme design and a feasibility proposal and proposed costs, etc had to be delivered within three months. At the end of this period the project had to be approved during a phase one stage. Many individuals were involved such as the parks and gardens sub-committee that was made up of eleven cross-party members from the Council. Similarly, another eleven members of the client services committee were asked to make comment. The full Council of 51 members and members of the public within the City were invited to make comment upon the proposals and the feasibility report put forward by the consultants. The procurement team hoped that this consultation process amongst the wider population of the Council and the public in general could be conducted in one month. However, this entire process took until September/October 2000. Once comments had been collated the documents were sent out to the necessary decision makers within one week of a planned meeting to finalise the way ahead. A further four months passed during which the complete design was settled. The competitive tendering process was to be applied in February 2001. It was envisaged that the potential contractors would be offered a three-week period to complete the tender exercise, after which there would be a contractual and legally binding contract when bonds would be required from contractors awarded the contract. A further eleven months would be set aside for work to be completed on the project. The City Council would evaluate decision on the award of the contract to a contractor on the basis of a 'best value' approach.

The contract 'brief' itself would contain a traditional approach seeking an architect, a quality surveyor and structural engineer and of course managing director services for the project. However, after assessing the potential of the market it was decided to use a more advanced approach and procure the project development through an all-in service. A procurement partner was to be chosen by the City Council to work alongside them through the project. The tender documents set out proposals for the design of the café at the crematorium contained in the consultation report that was passed to the contractors to plan a proposed programme of completion of the work on the project. There was scope for the contractor and the client (City Council) to manage the consultation services required for running the programme. The project manager from the contractors would responsible for the entire performance. After the tender documents had been issued to four companies the City Council expected that the contractors would contact them about the specification and the conditions surrounding the work. However, only one company made contact with some specific queries on the specification itself and the interpretation of it. After the close date of the tender had expired the procurement manager made an initial evaluation and realised that one company seemed to have misinterpreted the requirement and so this company was withdrawn from further consideration. There was quite a difference in the price submitted by the other two companies. These remaining two firms were interviewed to try to determine the approach that the company would use if awarded the contract to team working and to discuss issues of delivery. In the final analysis the company which was not the cheapest was deemed to be capable of providing the better quality approach to the project, but the lower priced company could it was felt be sufficiently well managed by the City Council staff in terms of the performance that they gave to warrant the award going to them. Quality was a large aspect of the decision-making criteria. The consultants awarded the contract had the majority of the team members required to operate the programme within the company and the others needed to manage the interior design were to be employed. The contract was then off and running.

During the course of the contract a decision was taken by the City Council to reduce the budget allocated to the project from £250, 000 to a new figure of £200, 0000. This affected the specification for the project, the resource allocation data, the cost control measures and the environmental management of the project.

The first step was to organise a site visit and a meeting of the operations manager and the team took place to discuss the delivery of the service. Time scales were identified as important to the project. The design of the project was offered in three options. The café was to be constructed in the middle former garden area of the building and meant that plans had to remove the garden in favour of an internal structure to facilitate the requirements of a waiting area and the café. Option one was a flat-roof construction with new walls joining at the chapel with a gap to provide a barrier to noise transfer. Option two offered a sloping roof towards the chapel side of the building. The third option was the one that the City Council selected as it had a pitched roof with tiles that matched the existing roof tiles on the rest of the building. It also matched the lead section on another part of the building and had a good appearance. The building dimensions were curtailed by the size of the courtyard which was 20 metres by 20 metres. The crematorium manager had been consulted as to the average size of mourner groups. He wanted the waiting area to accommodate a minimum of 50 and a maximum of 100 people. If a provision of 25 seats was made for those who required seating in the waiting area, then it was felt that the more could be housed. Provision for a servery for mourners who might wish to have something hot to eat was designed into the design scheme however it was suggested that this might be difficult to achieve. The building work was progressing from Monday to Friday however there was increasing internal pressure to speed the completion work up. The crematorium manager felt that the disruptions to the services had to be reduced. There was no cremation work permitted at the crematorium on Sundays however, if the building work was continued at night and on Saturdays, this might help. The contractor consented to undertake these new working arrangements but at a higher cost. The contractors requested some information about the new completion term to build the new area. Considerations about the buildability had now to be made. Higher costs were being incurred through the changes requested by the crematorium manager but the contractors thought that there were possibilities to look at the building plan and to procure materials differently to save monies. The implications of this were that the project could be continued maintaining the same quality approach as originally agreed and there could be approval given for the designs.

Role of the Procurement in the Organisation

The procurement team at the Belfast City Council have been forward thinking in the approach to much procurement in Belfast. In regard to this project the procurement team have been central to the new approach taken to the management of the contract. The design issues and the responsibilities for them lie ultimately with the Council. However, the procurement team are not only aware of the delicacy involved in the entire process of researching and developing the requirements within this contract but have been instrumental in designing the new facility in an appropriate and timely manner.

Conclusions

This contract was described by the City Council as one that required considerable emphasis upon design issues not only in terms of the building work extensions but also in terms of establishing the exact requirements in an unusual environment. Whilst the responsibilities of Belfast City Council are wide and various the issues that the case highlights are not those normally expected to be those dealt with necessarily by the City Council in the course of everyday procurement business. Nevertheless, the contracts team consulted widely to determine the special criteria important in this case. The topic of death and funerals is one that people invariably find difficult to discuss. Religious and cultural norms strongly influence the form of funeral rites. Thus, many of the people who might use the crematorium have specific views and stances on what should or should not be included in the facilities there. The City Council found it difficult to determine what facilities might be required at such an establishment. The delicate matter of who to ask about the facilities was one of the first issues under consideration. The response to the research undertaken by consultants and what the majority of the general public in this environment expects, naturally affects the acceptability of the services offered by the City Council at the crematorium. The City Council is concerned with the wishes of its population and also with the practicalities of managing the business of burial or cremation of the dead. The business at the crematorium is conducted within these confines and is a serious practical service provided to the greater population of Northern Ireland. Changes to or improvements in the environment of this business must be managed sensitively but still must allow the practical work to be conducted effectively. There were many different factors to be considered in the development of the waiting area that would not have presented themselves as so important had they have been provided elsewhere, certainly those in other Council-run buildings. Issues such as colour scheme, sound, music, access, privacy, harmony, emotion, and ambience may have been considered in the context of the development of a private sector café facility at any location. However, they would not have the same level of potential to cause upset although they may prove important from the perspective of a successful business. The contract design was a balance between the practical factors of the business processes in hand and the need to manage the aesthetics, specification, cost and constraints surrounding the acceptable provision of the service required.

Apart from the specification itself for the seemingly straightforward provision of a waiting area with catering facilities the City Council used a more forward-thinking contractual arrangement where the contractor provided an all-in service for the management of the project across all spheres of architectural, engineering and interior design work. The strengths of the procurement approach lay in the consideration of design issues early on in the project's concept development and in the partnering arrangement developed with the contractors who proved to be instrumental in cost reduction on the budget as the programme of delivery of the work was necessarily speeded up to reduce disruption to the overall service delivery at the crematorium.

Lessons Learnt

- Early consideration of design criteria is essential in determining requirements especially in relation to sensitive environments.

- Consultation with many different stakeholders involved with the procurement is important, particularly those working with or in the environment. In this contract there was a need to take into account both the practical concerns of those operating at an operational level within the crematorium as well as the needs of those mourners using the facilities in difficult and stressful circumstances from a personal perspective. If the Council had not researched the needs and discussed these with the 'workers' within the situation they would not have determined that in fact that the two groups (mourners and workers) had actually opposing requirements.

- An understanding of the circumstances surrounding the contract is important.

Case Synopsis

This case study was developed with the cooperation of the Belfast City Council. This case explores the practical development of a new waiting area with catering facilities at the crematorium in Northern Ireland. It on first appearance seemed to be a straightforward extension of the existing building and a new service provided by the Council. However, it actually proved fraught with complications that had to be managed in a particular way to ensure that the environmental issues, emotions and rites of individuals were preserved. Some interesting aspects were highlighted such as attempting to manage the unpredictable behaviours of people in mourning experienced by crematorium staff. The balance between practicalities and sensitivities in the development of the requirement tested the procurement and consultants.

The case sets the scene of the contract in the aims and role of the Belfast City Council and maps the developments of the contract through public sector competitive tendering regulations. The main benefit of examining this contract was to reveal the considerable design factors that exposed themselves as more research was undertaken and more stakeholders became involved. Seemingly unlikely factors had to be considered in the development of the requirements. There was an advanced approach taken to the award of the contract that differed from the norm in contracts of this nature. Whilst these are not fully explored in the case, it is clear that through the central management approach adopted for the contract that benefits in coordination and cost reduction were achieved.

Teaching and Learning Objectives

- To provide students with the opportunity to understand a case relaying best practice in the public sector procurement arena that explicitly incorporates design concepts early in its procurement strategy.
- To provide students with the basis for a discussion on the procurement path taken and the importance of design to both the product, service and the supply chain behind it all.
- To help students understand areas of synergy between design criteria for the development of new products and the procurement criteria for the development of sound procurement decisions.
- To explore the importance of involving key stakeholders in the procurement process throughout.

Main Issues Raised

- Consideration of design concepts
- Consideration of the impact of design upon the identification of need
- Consideration of design upon the finished procurement contract

- Consideration of procurement decision criteria
- Consideration of the importance of external and internal interface in the development of the requirement for procurement.

Specific Questions

1. Consider how design factors have featured in the planning of strategic procurement planning.

2. Discuss the contrast in sensitivity in the design of the cafe because it was to be based in the crematorium with the logistical issues of providing a vital service.

3. Identify the involvement of the various stakeholders in this case study process and explain the role that they played in the development of final framework.

4. Draw a flow diagram to show the stages of involvement of these stakeholders through the development of the framework process.

The Approach Taken

The case was approached from the perspective of design issues and how they have been integrated into the procurement strategy of this contract within the Belfast City Council. The full approach in terms of questioning and method for the development of the case study has been incorporated into the chapter of introduction in this text. The Pugh Model of Design Boundaries has been used to identify the main elements considered in new product design and those most pertinent to criteria for making decisions for various procurements throughout both the private and public sectors. This model was described at the outset of the interview for the collection of data for this case study. It was also discussed throughout the case study research to help identify the extent to which the design and procurement factors mesh together in the development of a new product where the innovation of suppliers is required to ensure that the end product is suitable for the purpose designated for it.

Chapter 4
Government Purchasing Card Case Study

Introduction

This case study follows the development of the government procurement card (GPC) concept through to departmental banking contracts being let in one department, that of Trade and Industry (DTI). A central approach was made to Visa by the HM Treasury's cross-government team for a Visa-based purchasing and payment card to be operated through its five issuing banks. The government procurement card is one effort to modernise and improve the efficiency and value for money of services for the taxpayer. The government procurement card contract is offered as an excellent model for the design of a government-wide service and of a collaborative and sharing of best practice that can deliver cost savings and value for money. This procurement approach had major impacts upon buying goods and services in government and on the culture of the organisation and how the government departments organise their payment processes. External to the government this procurement contract had major impact on suppliers of products and services to government as they had to adapt their processes to meet the new requirements and often change their own systems of acceptance of orders and payment methods too. This contract was seen as very much a mechanism to improve the way purchases are made within the context of the government. It was not seen as a way to fix or solve problems but as a spanner in a toolbox.

The government procurement card has been operating in government departments since 1998 when the then Central Unit Procurement (CUP) decided that they would develop a national procurement card. Research was done in the MoD on the cost of small-value items. An item such as a padlock that was priced at 98p actually cost £73.50 to purchase using the ordering, payment and invoicing system traditionally used in the government. Armed with such information the CUP approached the National Audit Office to develop a purchasing process for small-value items, as the current system was not cost effective. The business environment today is one of a cashless society where the need for money in notes and coins is reducing. The political debate around the denoted currency for Britain as the pound sterling or euro also affected the focus on using a procurement card rather than order systems to procure goods and services. The advances in technology and trans-national and global procurement and supply also heightened the need to consider smoother methods for ordering and payment. This was where the concept of the procurement credit card was developed. A process of tendering through the European Union using the public sector procurement regulations was undertaken. Institutions such as Visa, MasterCard, American Express and Diners were engaged in the process of offering a procurement credit card style arrangement. The CUP wanted a system of charging the small-value purchases to a card rather than using the typical ordering, payment and invoicing system that evidently added cost rather than value to the purchase. This new approach was not be a credit card system in the traditional way that procurement cards of this nature are known. It was not the intention of the government to allow credit upon the procurement card nor long running debt where interest would be paid upon purchases made on it.

As a result of the tendering exercise, the Visa institution was deemed to be the most appropriate organisation to provide the backing for the banking system behind the cards, by the lead departments and government agencies involved, ie the Northern Ireland Office and HM

Treasury. The role of Visa within the system is to set standards and maintain the infrastructure that underpins the authorisation and transaction processing. Visa in joining forces with HM Treasury has produced a simpler and more cost-effective method to purchase and pay for low-value goods and services.

A master agreement was made between HM Treasury and Visa to facilitate the use of the procurement card in a much cheaper way for the government on these small-value purchases. In the deal that was made between the government and Visa, three days consultancy from KPMG Ltd was offered to support departments in examining their facility's management procurement where most of the low-value items were purchased. Areas such as moving partitions or key cutting were prime targets to reduce the costs of procurement on this new procurement card approach. A local bank had to be identified for managing the accounts and issuing the cards for the government departments; this was to be decided by each department or agency individually.

The DTI Procurement Card Story

KPMG undertook consultancy in the DTI to cut out the ordering process in the department. A time and motion study was done which showed that introducing the card system could make a saving of £14 per transaction. Most of the identified savings were on the payment side of the transaction rather than the cost of the item itself. The number of, and monies that were spent on, invoices for such products as stationery ran into hundreds. It was envisaged that these would be reduced to one monthly statement through the new banking approach in the new procurement card system. Whilst the Visa Company was the main institution for management of the transactions and monies, there needed to be a bank adopted for the card issue. The DTI had to make a decision as to which bank to use. The five banks that operated under the Visa institution were Nat West, Midland, Bank of Scotland, Barclays and Ulster Bank. These were all interviewed after giving a presentation to the DTI procurement team. The banks operating the system and issuing these procurement cards did not charge for the use of the card but they were able to gain on the charges made to merchants for using them. The merchants whilst paying more charges to the banks would gain more, as they would benefit from the reduced payment times from government as a result of the new system. Each bank was required to make a presentation on the commercial terms that they offered. It was important for the DTI to see and speak to those people with whom they might work on this new system of payment. Barclays Bank impressed the DTI most and thus was chosen as the DTI bank to issue their procurement card. The other banks were debriefed on their performance and why they failed to be selected for the current contract. A pilot scheme for the introduction of the new approach to procuring low-value items was set up within three of the directorates in the DTI. The trial lasted for three months at first and then was reviewed to determine if the process was actually providing the savings projected by the research. A focus on the stationery items where some two million pounds was spent annually was deemed to be a good place to begin the process. The DTI also recognised that as the new system of payment would reduce the costs of payments to them it would also allow the suppliers involved with the DTI to reduce their paperwork and take less time in the processing of orders and invoices too. The suppliers would benefit from increased cash flow as a result and so the DTI sought reductions in the price of goods sold to them by these suppliers, seeking the reductions in costs for suppliers to be passed on to them.

Procurement Card Processes

As a start, 24 to 30 new DTI corporate cards were issued. A system of operation was developed to ensure the trial would be measurable.

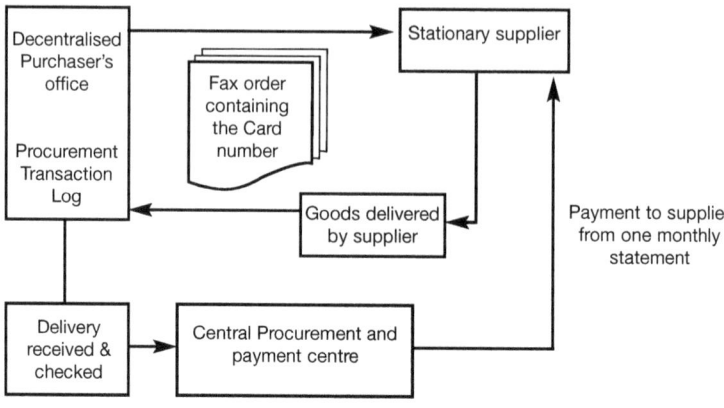

The programme for procurement cards has been rolled out over the last year and a half. Some 450 cards are now used in the DTI.

In the past year there has been in excess of £1million spent using the procurement card system with an estimated saving on payment services within the DTI of £125,000. There were some job cuts with the new system but most of the staff formerly deployed on payment of invoices and expediting orders were re-deployed on more strategic procurement tasks within the Department or involved in the central payment system set up to ensure that the Visa bill was paid on a monthly basis. The potential for the card was suggested at between £7-8million.

The DTI are considered to be front-runners in the use of these procurement cards and in operating a product-wide system usage for the Department. The Department is using both types of approach, broadly that of lodged and corporate cards. The expenditure on the card is now measured as £400million and the DTI aim to reach the targeted potential for use of the card identified above as £8 million pounds. The Department already ran a similar card with another bank and credit agent, specifically for travel requirements. The DTI did not wish to reduce the effectiveness of their travel card nor jeopardise their contract with the travel card provider. The travel card system was based on a two-type approach. A lodged card system was provided to travel agents that allowed buyers to fax or email their requirements to the agent and be provided with travel and a monthly statement to arrange payment after checking the details. The other approach was where a corporate card was issued to individuals who travelled on a regular or frequent basis on business. Individuals paid hotel bills using DTI monies rather than their own money with the requirement to claim back expenses from the Department after completion of the business trip.

Further, a lodged procurement card was issued to an agency contracted by the DTI to provide them with temporary staff. This business represented some £4million and was based on a framework contract. Instead of the DTI placing orders with the agency for services and the agency invoicing the DTI, the agency have been given the DTI procurement card number and are able to raise a purchase on the number without the former level of paperwork.

A total saving in the year 2000 was calculated at £150,000. There is an incentive to the DTI to place more business on the card as more money spent attracts rebates from the bank. Included in this level of savings made last year the DTI also secured £25,000 as a rebate from the bank.

From suppliers' perspective, the procurement card utilisation by the government in general is an improvement in payment terms for them. As the paperwork level reduces less time is taken to process the payment. A transaction now using the procurement card can take as little as two to four days as opposed to the legal requirement for government that suppliers had to be paid within 30 days. The vast improvement in cash flow that this concept has introduced has boosted suppliers' performance. The use of the card system by suppliers attracts a three per cent charge to them, but this is more than offset by the cash flow situation and the reduction of costs in operating administrative procedures and so is an attractive proposition. The caveat to using the procurement card and indeed accepting the card is that both parties need to be registered to use Visa. Not all suppliers particularly of items considered to be of lower value or classified by the DTI as small items can accept Visa transactions. To become registered and set up for working on Visa payments would cost suppliers some initial capital outlay. Traditionally, the VisaCard system was accepted by general merchants and retailers, whereas MasterCard tended to be accepted by plumbers and builders merchants and Amex tended to be accepted by the top end of the market.

Government Procurement Environment

At first some managers in the DTI were not sure of issuing procurement cards to all levels of staff. They were concerned that perhaps junior staff particularly might abuse the card system. However, the bank discussed the level of controls that could be placed upon the card both on range and level of expenditure per transaction and this eased some of the worry. As discussed two main levels of control on the card usage was adopted, firstly the limit per transaction of no more than £500 would be sufficient incentive to prevent abuse as no member of staff would be prepared to lose their job as a consequence of buying such a relatively low-value item on the card. As the card system operated on a statement basis and was checked and verified each month any abuse of the card would be easily detected and therefore the 'fraud' exposed readily. The card itself was programmed to cease to operate if it was used more than twelve times continuously as an additional fraud prevention measure. Secondly, the necessity to maintain a transaction log by each authorised user would also send specific signals for, and provision of, the use of procurement cards. An argument was put forward by advocators of the cards that if someone wanted to abuse the buying system that could just as easily place a paper-based order and secure the goods or services that they wanted. The risk therefore to abuse using the procurement card was deemed to be no more than using any other buying system. There had only been one reported case of fraud using the card in the wider government service where someone purchased a football jersey using the government procurement card; this resulted in the person being sacked as the measures for detection of such fraud were in place and proved to work. Nevertheless, the DTI had the agreement of the internal audit function within the Department and the National Audit Office and so started to convert anti-card people to using the card.

The potential to use the procurement card to purchase on the Internet was great. Many contracts have not been set up on the Internet but some opportunities exist to buy books through companies such as Amazon.com.

Security for procurement across government is a major issue using the procurement card in a much greater way than the former order-based approach. To inform members of staff about security and restrictions on using the procurement card in the course of DTI business an intranet site was developed listing well-known suppliers and processes, etc. One government procurement card has been reported lost but only two cases of incorrect use, both described as accidental spend, within the DTI have been reported, where one individual used their assigned government procurement card instead of their own private card whilst shopping. The mistake was noticed after the card had been swiped and was rectified immediately as a personal cheque was written for the amount to the DTI to cover the error. New control measures have been suggested for locking the card in safes rather than carrying the card about on a daily basis. Each card has an annual expiry date so there is a requirement to reissue each card annually. Similarly as members of staff leave the Department they must surrender the procurement card. As new members join the Department then they must apply for a procurement card if they are to be authorised to use one. There are new issues of procurement cards regularly to meet this need. There has to be strict security surrounding the issue and surrender of cards.

Features of the Procurement Card

The main use of the card is on general goods and services such as for training courses, and first aid products, stationery etc. Expenses for members of staff such as for travel were not included on the corporate card.

The Visa procurement card can be set up electronically to bar specific product types from the card that would then stop buyers purchasing items using this method of procurement. If a buyer attempted to use the card for products that had been barred by the authoriser, the purchase would be rejected and the transaction aborted. The DTI had the opportunity to utilise all 36 of the merchant categories set out by the Visa institution to identify the goods and services bought by all businesses. The DTI surveyed these categories and sought to restrict as few as possible to allow the full potential of the card to permeate through the Department and its expenditure. Some categories such as travel were excluded as discussed above and others such personal services were deemed outside of the required procurement scope for the Department. The cash withdrawal facility on the procurement card was barred so there was no personal indicative number attributed to the government Visa system, as this was not required either. The categorisation system allowed the card authoriser to choose which products and services they would permit for purchase under a specific card. However, having selected a range of categories identified as appropriate the DTI realised that some of them were unnecessary and caused excess billing sheets to be produced and so were reduced over time to a more realistic number representing the most popular items procured in the Department. Therefore through an electronic chip in each card the range of purchases permitted could be varied as required. For instance the buyers in charge of a furniture budget would be permitted access to this type of product purchase, limited by expenditure levels of course, but could be barred from using the card for other purchases such as consumable computer items. The categorisation proved useful to companies in general for this control but also for budget measurement purposes.

Generally speaking the main control on the card for the DTI lies in limiting the expenditure per transaction to no more than £500 and a figure of £1000 per month. However, there are exceptions to this, as various requirements demand a higher limit placed upon it, for example, the training department are permitted to spend up to £20,000 per month.

Customers

Each member of staff who was authorised to use a government procurement card has to apply for an individual card identified with a unique 16 digit number, through the bank. They are subject to Visa checking procedures and served with a limit upon expenditure as designated by the Department. The limit placed upon the use of the card can be raised or ceased within two hours of notification to the bank. Only the authorised user can use each card. Ninety percent of the procurement cards are open to most procurement categories.

Aesthetics

The aesthetic design of the procurement card was of importance to the DTI as well as security for the usage of the card. As a government department there were certain protocols to be observed in the appearance of the card. A striking black plastic card design was selected for the general procurement card. Barclays also offered a silver corporate card that offered more protection to the user in terms of free insurance to be used whilst travelling. The card design had to include details of the department using the card and identify the individual cardholder along with the card number. Several iterations of the card have been designed as minor changes to the layout of names and department titles were incorporated. The DTI is a dynamic Department that re-organises itself to best serve the needs of the Department. This proved to be an issue for the card designers, as there needed to be a card describing the current directorate make up within the Department. Originally when the card was developed the DTI had nine different directorates; now these nine directorates have been merged at the bank and a new design has been authorised to accommodate the structural changes.

Design Advances in the Use of the Procurement Card

The DTI set up a designated website for their contracted suppliers to place the products and services that are available for purchases under the various contractual agreements. New catalogues for all manner of products that have been developed through the central government tendering legislation are identified on the site. Specific passwords to facilitate, restrict and control entry to the website have been developed for procurement cardholders. The entire procurement process has attracted bigger discounts for government buyers as reduced costs are passed on in the price of goods displayed upon the website. The DTI are working on a 'shopping basket' approach to buying on the website similar to those that one would find on a website such as Tesco where the buyer can browse various shelves or departments in the catalogue and collect purchases as required and then make one transaction for all the items selected. As this is a new approach for government and has the potential to provide a marketing avenue for selected suppliers to list their products under the contract more suppliers need to undertake the path to being able to accept Visa transactions.

Benefits of the Procurement Card

The introduction of the GPC offered departments significant process cost reductions whilst maintaining control over expenditure. Whilst devolving the activity of purchasing low-value items to the cost centre budget holder and the authorised procurement card user who manage each low-value purchase, the Department procurement teams can focus on higher-value items and on more strategic activities.

Overall with this new system there will be fewer requisitions, fewer purchase orders, less invoicing and fewer invoice queries. Many of the individual order transactions will be consolidated and payments will be issued on one monthly statement instead of multiple payments made to many suppliers.

Suppliers will benefit from an improved payment cycle and improved cash flow. Using this system will also will reduce their paperwork and a lesser need for credit control mechanisms will be the result. It is envisaged that the system will promote stronger customer relationships.

Another advantage of the card is that the high level of expenditure brings rebates on use of the card. Government departments also had been set a target, by the HM Treasury, to achieve 90% electronic systems in their departments. This new procurement system helped them to meet this target.

In addition the DTI do not have to use their onerous resource-based accounting (RAB) system to raise orders as the procurement card system permitted a legitimate bypassing of the accounting system straight through to the accounts payable ledger which received the orders eventually on the former system after entry and transfer through the RAB. This was a significant advantage in terms of administrative management of the accounting practices overall.

The data produced by the banks and the ability to compare to transaction logs have revealed mistakes in pricing by the suppliers which may not have been picked up in the former system. The new role for procurement is therefore gearing up the suppliers to electronic trading and the extrapolation of information on trends in expenditure, etc.

Problems with the Procurement Card

The problems associated with managing low-value purchases are common to both the public and private sectors. Mostly they relate to the cost of purchases being too high relative to the value of the procurement. The problem that the procurement card system sought to address was to reduce the workload for the accounts department on low-value orders and high levels of orders. All of the cards held by DTI staff members are distributed across various departments. Whilst each cardholder maintains a local transaction log, the monthly statement for each card must be sent centrally to the procurement unit. The payments for all cards for the DTI are paid within 14 days of receipt of the bill. The task then to allocate the various payments for different products and services categories on each card to each budget holder is undertaken by the central procurement unit. This is often a difficult task as it is not easy to attribute costs to actual accounts in the various functional business areas within the DTI. The DTI have identified an internal system whereby the central procurement unit allocate all 450 card accounts to their respective cost centre budget accounts and then each budget account holder must reallocate the expenditure to products and services categories so as to record the departmental expenditure more accurately. The cost centres throughout the Department are identified on the monthly Visa statement and are therefore easy to attribute the procurement card expenditure to. The bank has the facility to produce the bill on floppy disk and so makes the task of interrogating the data contained on the bill easier. There is computer software available to enable the procurement department to feed the data directly onto departmental ledgers, however this is very expensive and has not yet been purchased by the DTI.

The categorisation of the goods and services can cause problems. The nature of any categorisation relies on conformity to detail and strict adherence of the boundaries for the category classification. The DTI found that one of its staff using a procurement card approached the books and stationery business WH Smith to purchase some diaries. The card transaction failed as invalid usage. Upon investigation of the incident the company had been designated as a travel agent by the Visa institution, because as part of its business it did actually sell travel. The member of staff's card had been barred from purchasing travel and so this was why the card was rejected. No illegal or fraudulent action had occurred in the use of the card but the designation of the company as a travel agent rather than a stationery supplier had barred the purchase of diaries. Thus the control system in this instance had prohibited a legitimate purchase. This incident raised issues about the need to open all categories rather than blocking or barring some.

The DTI had as explained already been using a travel card for some time. There had not been much use of this card as only specific individuals within the Department who travelled regularly used it. As the introduction of the Visa card system for low-value transactions was proving effective and efficient there was a question now of why the Visa card which attracted a large rebate for high level use should not be used for all procurements without exceptions. The DTI procurement team have prepared a submission to request permission to open the Visa card to travel.

Management of the Government Procurement Card

The central procurement team are responsible for the payment of the Visa bill and the management of the information that these bills and the bank provide. The procurement team on a monthly basis prepare a booking statement to transfer the payments recorded on the Visa bill to specific cost centre accounts. A floppy disk is supplied on a monthly basis containing data on the suppliers with which the purchases were made, and on the cardholders' patterns of purchases made. The central procurement team manage this information to determine what is purchased, when and by whom over the monthly period and collate this expenditure annually.

The entire process has been running for two years and is proving a success in terms of savings for the government budget overall.

Conclusions

The procurement of a government procurement charge card contract is put forward as an excellent model of procurement of a collaborative service that is designed for use in many different circumstances by different levels of staff with varying responsibilities. There was much research into the benefits of such a card with the various banking institutions and credit/charge card system managers. The central government team generating the contract had to use the EC procurement legislation to build the competition for the contract but once this was established a provider was selected with which the basic contract could be developed. Each department that was to use the contract played a part in the development of the service that it required from the individual banks that supplied the accounts and issued the procurement cards. Each department was able to design the system and the appearance of the procurement card as they wished. In the context of design issues there were important factors to consider in relation to the environment within government and the culture. Similarly the security factors and control mechanisms that had to be put in place were important. Company constraints and market responsibilities featured heavily in the decisions made on the procurement card contract. The savings that were achieved by using the card were as expected from the research undertaken.

Lessons Learnt

- The more research undertaken prior to the development of the service contract the more effective the contract became.

- Understanding the environment in which the contract was to operate was important in terms of working the new procurement card system and designing the card and the service behind it.

- Consultation with the many stakeholders involved in the procurement and design is essential, in this case with the bank, the managing institutions, the suppliers, the potential cardholders, finance, accounts, procurement team, etc.

Specific Questions

1. Consider the GPC case study in the light of the Pugh Model of Design Boundaries provided in the introduction to this book, to determine how

many of the cited 'design' and 'procurement' criteria were considered in the development of this governent procurement card.

2. Consider how important the inclusion of these criteria is to the success of the entire project.

3. Identify the stake holders in this case study and explain the role they played in the development of the final framework.

Chapter 5
Driving Standards Agency Driving Test Theory Case Study

Introduction

This case study looks at the development of the Driving Theory Test, at the Driving Standards Agency (DSA), that now forms part of the two-part road-driving test in Great Britain, consisting of a separate theory and practical driving test, for which they are responsible. Prior to this period British drivers had to pass a practical driving test and a theory element conducted by examiners orally at the end of this practical driving test, to be legally permitted to drive on the roads.

The DSA began the development of this theory test contract and in 1996 a transition period for the two-part driving test was initiated. The test has progressed from a written test in 1996 to a touch screen theory test in January 2000. This research tracks the development of this very complex design-rich theory test contract and explains the best practice process that was utilised by the DSA in the development of the end product – the two-part driving test.

The DSA is an executive agency of the Department of the Environment, Transport and the Regions and a member of the Driver, Vehicle, and Operator Group that provides a service to drivers and vehicle operators. The DSA maxim is: ' "Safe driving for life" and we endeavour to influence drivers' behaviour for the better throughout their driving career and cut novice driver accidents by concentrating on early years of driving in the run up to their test and the period immediately after'.

The primary aims of the DSA are: road safety through improving driving standards; testing drivers, motorcyclists and driving instructors fairly and efficiently through the theory test and practical driving test; maintaining the registers of Approved Driving Instructors and Large Goods Vehicle Instructors; and supervising training to learner motorcyclists. The DSA adheres to the government road safety strategy that has been formulated around three key new road casualty reduction targets: death of adults and children; serious injury of adults and children; and slight injury. In addition to this the DSA is also involved with the European Commission to ensure harmonisation of changes to minimum requirements for the theory and practical driving test throughout Europe.

The Agency operates out of Nottingham as a main headquarter base, on a trading fund of some £80million per annum and is fully funded through income fees and revenue from other road safety initiatives. There are over 400 practical test centres and administrative offices in cities such as London, Newcastle, Edinburgh, Cardiff and Birmingham.

Driving Theory Test Background

In 1989 the then Department of Transport published a consultation paper, explaining the implications of the recently published European Driving Test Directive. There was a cited requirement for each European member state to adopt minimum requirements for driving tests that had to include a theory test that tested candidates on their knowledge and skills in exhibiting behaviour commensurate with driving motor vehicles. The Directive was eventually ratified into national legislation in Britain in 1991. In the past the driving examiner would ask candidates six questions on the Highway Code, after their practical test. However, the European Union required a more rigorous test: the theory test is separate to the practical test; it requires a formal examination paper, and a record of results to be retained. It has been recognised that the former system of limiting the number and range of questions on an oral basis restricts the number and form that questions can take. Whilst the new EU legislation required a separate theory test there were neither instructions nor process guidelines as to how to achieve such a test. Some topic areas were suggested in the Directive, but how these were implemented in each member state was left to each country.

There were some standards identified in the Directive however; the emphasis was placed upon improving new and young drivers' performance. The view was very much to achieve 'safe drivers for life'.

Recent DSA statistics on road accidents revealed that drivers between 17 and 21 years represented around 10% of all licence holders but that they actually caused 20% of all accidents on the roads. This age group, the new and young drivers, was responsible for one quarter of the road fatalities. The ethos behind the separate theory test was try to improve the road safety record of new and young drivers through making them better prepared for road situations by ensuring that they have the requisite knowledge and understanding before they receive a licence to drive on those roads. The DSA see a strong link between the separate theory test and safer driving.

The theory test, introduced as a separate test on 1 July 1996, was a multiple-choice-based written examination designed to meet the stated requirements of the European Union Second Directive on Driver Licensing. Alongside the creation of the theory test, in 1999, the practical driving test was also revised expanding the test to 35 minutes' duration during which the candidate was exposed to a greater variety of road conditions. This test incorporated new pass criterion, for example the number of driver faults constituting failure was now 16 or more. Subsequently, there was a decrease in the pass rates for driving tests between 1996 and 1999. There were various reasons for this such as the nature of the practical test being longer and more demanding. There was a decrease in the number of pass rates for the theory test over this period from 61.8% in 1996 to 61.4% in 1999/2000 for car drivers. During this time there was an increase in the number of questions that must be answered correctly to pass the test and the introduction of additional questions. There was an increase noted though to pass rates once candidates adjusted to the new standards and approach. In January 2000 a new computerised touch-screen version of the theory test was introduced.

The Driving Theory Test Contract Approach

A new policy division was set up in DSA known as the Road Safety Division to oversee the management of driving tests.

In 1994, the driving theory test contract was developed in several parts: test development and service provision for delivery of the test. The intended commencement date for the test was 1 July 1996; therefore the contracts for development of the tests were created in 1993 and awarded in 1994. The contract for service provision behind the test itself was let in Spring 1995.

The contracts for this area were by nature going to be very complex and required detailed specification and understanding of the need from the outset. The DSA engaged with 40 suppliers in a bidders' workshop to provide presentations on the requirements and any likely problems or challenges envisaged throughout the process. There was a possibility to form consortia for some of the contractors who may have found this contract within their skill base but outside of their management in terms of size and commitment, etc. Those 40 initial suppliers were reduced to 20 for the purposes of tendering efficiency and effectiveness.

The DSA had to make it clear that in any contract awarded for this procurement they would own the intellectual property of the system and the development work, as the DSA would pay for all of the work. Once the development took place any further work would be the joint property of those involved. The DSA also made it clear in the workshops held with potential bidders and suppliers that a constraint had been placed upon those companies involved in providing driving lessons or those offering instruction for the driving of buses and coaches. Whilst the DSA recognised that this might distort the market they felt it was necessary that companies could not be accused of having a vested interest nor have a connection with a service provider who was involved in passing or failing tests for drivers of any kind.

One contract consisted of the creation and development of the car drivers' theory test itself. The National Foundation for Education Research (NFER) was engaged to perform these duties through a competitive tender exercise in 1994. A further contract with the NFER was awarded in 1995 to develop similar tests for learner lorry, bus and coach drivers. Initially they were required to undertake research to develop a bank of theory tests questions and papers of equivalent difficulty. A deadline for this creation and development work to deliver final test papers to DSA was January 1996 for the car drivers' test and April 1996 for the other drivers' tests. Similarly a schedule for the development of the motorbikers' theory test was planned for 1997.

The NEFR opted for a multiple-choice approach, as this would be more easily operated and marked. The subject matter for the questions was set out in the Directive in the form of topics to be covered. Each question would have four possible answers only one of which would be the correct answer from that selection. A bank of 600 questions was developed which made up a series of 20 tests. These tests would be made available to the DSA who would take responsibility for the rotation of the tests throughout the various centres and for individuals taking the test. It was critical to determine the time duration for the theory test that was set at 35 minutes. There was a concession of time for those candidates with special needs who would be allocated double the normal time period for completion of the test.

As part of the contract for the creation and development of the theory test there was a requirement on the NFER to trial the tests. A trial of some existing drivers who had already passed their test was to determine the appropriateness of the questions, the time it would take them to complete the test and the level of difficulty in the questions. Indeed there was an interest in the framing of the questions and whether any ambiguity had crept in to the questions offered throughout the test. The trial was run on existing drivers rather than those wishing to take the test so as to assess the questions and approach to the test taken by the NFER under normal circumstances. Statistics gathered through the trials showed the level of ambiguity in the questions and exposed those that caused problems through the test. Each question was also given a difficulty rating.

Much work was done in the design of the test papers and how the candidates taking the test would perceive these papers. Ergonomics was taken into account in the development of the papers so that it took the form of multiple pages but the question and answers were contained in one booklet. To make assessment of the tests, from a marking perspective, the questions and answers needed to be laid out in a manner that permitted the optical scanner to pick up the marks on the answers readily. There was a necessary trade-off between the machinery required to electronically mark the papers and the design of the questions and answers method. The DSA examined the paper design and the process as a whole and took the view that there would be more added value in using electronic methods of marking and assessment and that failure by candidates to insert the correct mark in the answer box on the test paper would have to be tackled through human intervention as exception marking rather than to have the entire test process hand marked. In the choice of electronic versus manual marking there were issues to be weighed up of time and volume of tests undertaken to consider and also the number required, availability of, and costs of human markers for the test if manually completed. For an additional fee candidates could request same-day marking of their test paper.

Aesthetics too proved important in the design approach taken by the DSA and NFER in terms of presentability and professional appearance of the paper itself. Issues such as making the paper appeal to the candidate and ensuring that it was easy to read, see and that the pictures used to represent symbols and signs or even police cars and lorries are actually typical of what the general public might see on a daily basis. There needed to be a way of making sure for instance that candidates turned the page or did actually follow the question format to the end of the paper, ie not missing out questions which might then mean a fail mark. The back page of the test paper, it was found after analysis of data, was often missed out by candidates undertaking the test and so the service providers were required by the DSA to insert a special message at the start of each test given by invigilators to emphasis the need to turn over to the last page.

Each test has a vehicle symbol on the front to demonstrate the type of test contained in the document such as a car for the car theory driving test and a motorbike for the motorbike test. As each test is offered in different languages there needs to be some method of designation of what language the given paper is in. This issue alone caused considerable problems and was accentuated when the test was developed using the multi-media tools. Software was extremely difficult to develop as the same layout and approach needed to be taken. Each paper needed to clearly look the same so that the perception of the material contained in the test was the same to each candidate no matter what language it was taken in. There was a view in the DSA that candidates might raise continuity and fairness issues in respect of the visible difference to each paper. The more languages the test paper is offered in the more complicated the translation issues for the DSA become. There is a facility for candidates to take a human translator into the test with them but purely for the purposes of repeating the question in the chosen language not to help the candidate to answer any questions. To this end there has to be a monitoring process in place to ensure correctness of actions during the test period. Candidates are invited in each test taken to indicate their choice of answer to a given question in a box by filling in the 'X' against the answer that they believed to be correct. If a mistake is made candidates are required to completely cover the wrongly chosen ' X' box and insert the new choice of answer.

An example of the questions posed and the expected approach to answering the question in the theory driving test is given below. Each paper is identified with a code reference number and a specific line characteristic positioned on the paper in line with the answer boxes indicates where the electronic marker needs to be to read the marks made for the answer. This feature helps align the papers for accurate assessment. It also helps to identify the inception errors picked up in the marking process by using the electronic optical scanning machine.

As the tests are marked electronically there is a right of appeal offered to each candidate and his or her test paper is kept for a six-month period after the test was undertaken.

Q1. You are invited to a pub lunch. You know that you will have to drive that evening. You are advised to

Mark one answer

a. ☒ avoid mixing your alcohol drinks

b. ☑ not drink any alcohol at all

c. ☒ have some milk before drinking alcohol

d. ☒ eat a hot meal with your alcoholic drink

Q2. What does this warning light on the instrument panel mean?

a. ☒ Mark one answer

b. ☒ Low oil pressure

c. ☒ Battery discharge

d. ☑ Braking system fault

e. ☒ Door open

The DSA, however, took responsibility for test maintenance, whereby test data provided by NFER would be analysed in terms of performance of specific papers and questions. It was the responsibility of DSA to weed out 'bad' questions or papers from the test series bank. They took on responsibility for writing and trailling new questions and issuing new test papers annually. The DSA will deliver the new questions or test papers once a year in March with the intention that these will be introduced into the bank of questions in July each year. DSA staff were sent on specific training programmes to develop the necessary skills to write questions for the test.

Once sufficient test papers had been satisfactorily developed the DSA handed them over to another contractor to provide services to continue the work towards test delivery.

A separate contract commencing in January 1996 was awarded on the basis of European Procurement Directives, negotiated procedure, for an extendable three-year period, to a provider of services as follows:

- Printing and distribution of the test papers, including the papers into the required languages of Welsh, Chinese, Bengali, Gujerati, Hindi, Punjabi and Urdu
- Booking appointments for candidates for the appropriate category of theory test and receiving and banking and accurately accounting for fee receipts for the test
- Refunding test fees to candidates in accordance with guidelines agreed with DSA
- Providing suitable premises for the delivery of the test
- Conducting the theory test itself, including invigilating the test and identification checks on participants
- Marking of test papers and the distribution of results to the candidates and the provision of results data to DSA
- Providing management information and other test data to DSA and the Department of Transport (now DETR).

The DSA worked out a process to deliver the service that is shown overleaf in diagrammatical format.

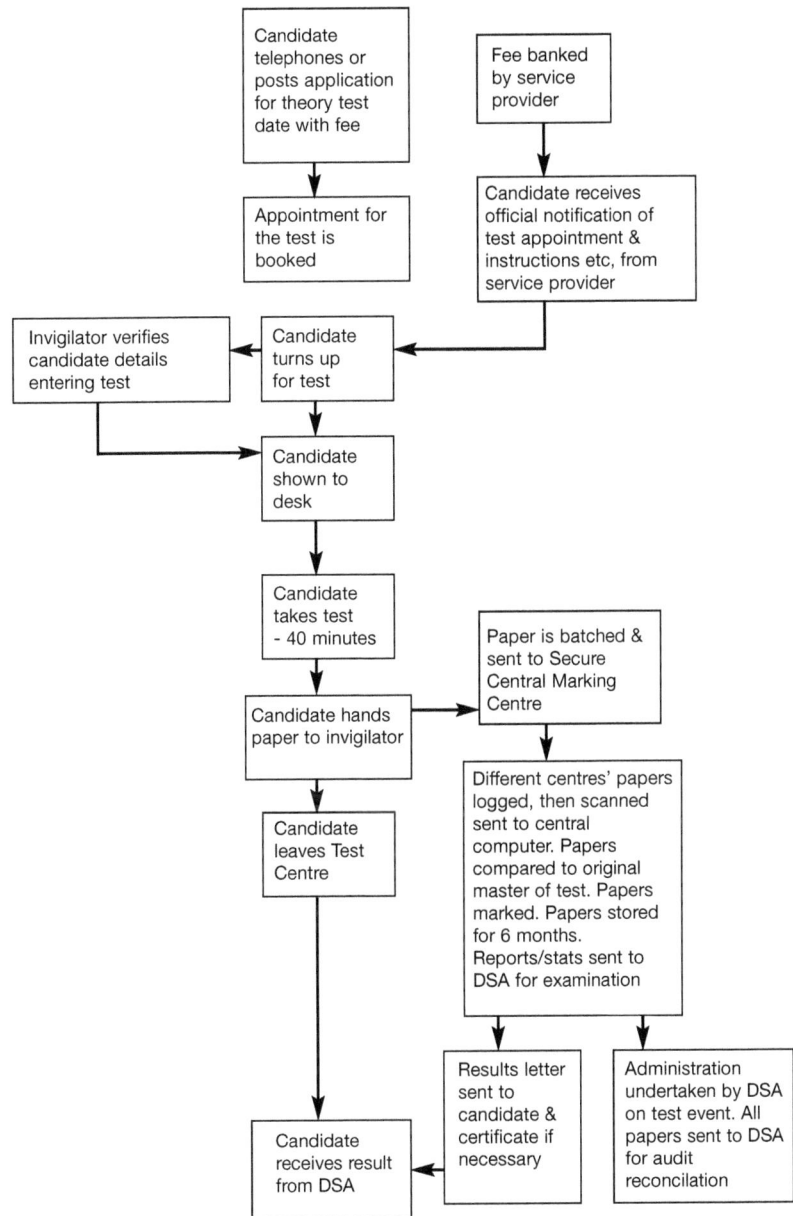

It was critical that the contracts for both development of the tests and service provision for delivery of test centres, etc allowed the smooth running of the entire test. The sequence of completion of the overall driving test was to be the theory test first then the practical test next, so this had an impact on the introduction date for the theory test to be in line with the ability to undertake the practical test. Failure to sequence these tests correctly might cause delays in the ability of members of the public to obtain a driving licence. This would not be acceptable.

The product cost to members of the public was very much a political issue and this needed to be reflected in the fees charged for the entire process of becoming legally able to drive. On average it was suggested in the National Audit Report in 1997 and by the DSA that it would cost something in the region of £400 to learn to drive with a DSA-recognised instructor; the cost of the practical test was set at £30 and the theory test and manual for it was to be set at £15; a total of £445. There was political pressure to reduce the fee for the driving tests to no more than £20. It has already been indicated in this study that the DSA are self-funding from the fees charged for the tests and other initiatives and so there is also great pressure on the level of service provision in running the tests that can be offered in terms of revenue gained for the tests. A trade-off between price paid and quality delivered was key in setting the correct or appropriate test delivery circumstances.

It was deemed important too by the DSA that accessibility to take the test in the designated centres should be easy. The centre established for the theory tests would be separate to where the candidate would register for the practical test. It was left to the contractor to determine whether to contract the use of local further education colleges or to set up dedicated test centres. Therefore many of the theory test centres are in town whereas the practical test centres are usually out of town. Research had been undertaken in the 1990s to determine how and over what distance members of the public travelled to undertake their tests. It was decided that there should be a test centre accessible within a maximum of a 20-mile radius to the larger populated areas.

Within the specification for the service provision there needed to be a stipulation for the contractor to ensure that no-one was allowed to sit the driving theory test without producing appropriate documentation such as a valid European driving licence. Embodied, too, in the specification for the service provision of test facilities was the requirement to consider the output for each test centre. Performance measures were based on contract service output, for instance, for distance from the main population areas, the level of transport accessibility, level of disabled access, availability of waiting areas and rooms, size and facilities in the test area, layout and spacing in the test areas for desking etc, measurement of the process used in running the examination/test including the invigilation tasks etc, the process for booking appointments and for marking the tests. Customer satisfaction was an important feature of the measures that were put in place. If customers were dissatisfied for some reason then a leaflet on what was open to them in seeking redress was produced. The candidates might have cause to complain over issues such as environmental noise, speed of answering complaints or indeed attitude of staff in any communications.

A large part of the service provision revolved around customer contact with the service provider to arrange test appointments and to answer queries. Targets were set out for the contractor in terms of telephone answering where 95% of all calls were to be answered in within 10 seconds of ringing in. The calls were tracked by the telephone switching equipment. Overall standards had to be maintained over a 24-month period or a liquidated damage clause came into effect through the terms of conditions of contract. To this end there were agreed between the parties a set of measurement and performance criteria for quality of service and technical issues, with minimum standards specified associated with lower price payments to the contractor. The assistance was sought in the development of the specified requirements for setting out the test room and invigilation was discussed with the Examination Board Awarding Bodies. The service provider too had to undertake research and produce specified data on pass marks achieved, pass rates and the quantity of tests that were taken in a given period. Statistics were produced for the first year of operation and there were between 1.2 million and 1.5 million tests conducted in that period. These statistics were derived from the number of applications requested. Exception reports were requested to expose facts, for instance one candidate failed the test 29 times, which could then be analysed. The tests were based on an educational level set for on average that of an eleven-year-old so by setting a lower educational standard the test would not be too hard.

The choice of service provider to execute the delivery of tests and centres was very important as the DSA wished to be seen as the front-line managers of the test and the members of the public taking the test would apply, pay, take and receive results etc through the DSA although the service provider would in actual fact undertake all of these duties. The service provider was in effect to be an invisible contractor meeting all the requirements but unknown to the public in their work. This was required for several reasons. Firstly the DSA needed to be the front-line body insofar as the public were concerned so as to protect the contractor and its reputation in respect of delivery of the service. Such a responsibility for the contractor might leave them open to attempts to defraud the driving test system; if they were unknown to the public this would then be an unlikely consequence of their working relationship. Secondly, the DSA had public sector responsibility to the European Union to carryout driving test legislation and take responsibility for the execution of this legislation. There were specified legal requirements under EU legislation to enforce and monitor the regulations pertinent to the theory test, ensure that satisfactory special needs facilities and equipment was available for those taking the test who were disabled, to provide for minority languages in the delivery of the tests, to ensure that the Highway Code was a central feature of the test and that those taking the tests should have driving manuals and good practice tips on taking the test and on driving. So much so that the DSA consulted with the Departmental lawyers to ensure that they could continue to fulfil their obligations under the law. This meant that whilst the day-to-day delivery of the test provision could be managed by a contractor the DSA still needed to be 'hands on' in the overall responsibility for the test cycle.

On-Screen Theory Test

The new on-screen theory test is a computerised test with multi-media features that permit candidates to touch the screen to complete the test rather than any typing or keyboard action. There was a deliberate decision to keep the term 'computerised' out of the description of the test innovation as this may cause some distress to members of the public wishing to take the theory test, through fear and unfamiliarity with computerisation, per se or due to a link associated with difficulty and complexity that might sit with computerisation.

In 1994 the DSA had considered using an on-screen test from the outset of the introduction of the theory test, and had spent some three months in seeking out and researching computerised testing. However, they were pressured at that time by MPs to pursue a written theory test as the costs of an on-screen one at that time were deemed to be preclusive. Once the DSA set this written system up they were immediately criticised as that system was said to be inflexible and that it did not reflect modern approaches to tests.

In 1997 the DSA set up a project team to research the concept of electronic testing more thoroughly. This time the pressure from MPs was for computerisation of the tests. By mid-1997 the project manager and the head of theory test policy division began a feasibility analysis. By late 1997 the project team began searching out other users of such testing programmes. They investigated the Australian computer testing software that offered a good solution. This system was used as a reference site and as a steer to evaluation processes. After speaking to two government departments in Australia and New Zealand they became aware of envisaged problems that using this computerised approach to testing might bring. These revolved around issues of candidate knowledge and use of technology and the development of a common language of communication. Whilst the DSA had thought of these issues when developing the written tests they appreciated that the computerised system might well escalate such problems. They sought to find out how multi-media tools would assist in the resolution of these matters. Sound was another main issue that needed to be incorporated adequately in the development work. Special needs features such as an on-screen video add-on and the ability to have the question repeated should it be needed were identified through this research as important developments. The DSA took the opportunity to link with suppliers who developed the American army skills test to determine why their particular screens were developed in the way they were.

DSA Approach to the Market

The DSA needed to research the market for knowledge for the development of the specific software that was required in this situation. The original company who had worked with DSA in the development of the first theory test system offered to upgrade their tests to a computerised system but there were legal and value-for-money criteria that had to be met by the DSA which necessitated a completely new tendering exercise. In addition to this the DSA needed to undertake a new tendering exercise as the development of the software system etc would be a new element of the delivery of the test provision. So separate contract approaches needed to be adopted for the development of software to run the test and for the amended approach to the service delivery behind the test delivery brought about by the change to computerisation of the test.

The DSA saw an opportunity, in the new tendering exercise, to embody required specification changes to the service provision circumstances that had been thrown up by actual delivery performance and issues that were not specified appropriately at the outset. The introduction of regulation changes such as a minimum cancellation period, a change in fee for the test and the parameters for determination of quick responses, an immediate response to test in terms of a pass or fail on completion of the test could also be made. Some of these issues had been exposed from customer satisfaction questionnaires and complaints voiced by candidates during calls to the service provider. Additions to the information provided for candidates could be included in the form of new targets for the provision of enhanced results and the use of first class post to communicate with customers. Originally, with the former system, candidates only received a pass or fail grade but with the development of the new system the equipment could provide a mark attained by each candidate of the total attempted questions which was 35. Many other service enhancements were formalised into the service provisions contract. There had been some 150 variations to the contract in the three-year period of the contract, as awareness of service responsibilities and clarification of circumstances for undertaking the test grew. There was a requirement for 20 additional test centres to be introduced to the contract system. These centres had been added as the result of MPs and customers lobbying for better and closer facilities in their specific geographical area. There were 138 centres in year one of the contract that was then increased by these additions. There was a recognition that the increased number of test candidates raised increased funds through fees and so service provision could also be enhanced.

Currently, NEFR still are engaged under contract to devise the test and assess the facility values for that test in terms of levels of difficulty etc. However, a new turnkey system was introduced in December 1999, although the booking office was available from November 1999, to cover the new provision of the service behind the delivery of the test. Existing employees working in the theory test centres were offered the opportunity to move across to the new company and this meant that the European legislation pertinent to transferring staff from one employer to another in the course of a contractual change was applied. This legislation is known as Transfer of Undertakings for Employees (TUPE). Whilst the DSA recognised the need to transfer the delivery of one service to another there were concerns as it had not been the original point of the exercise to necessarily utilise the same test centres as many of these did not prove suitable for computerised testing. The first computerised test took place on 4 January 2000.

Service Delivery Specification Developments

The specification work was completed by mid-1997 and the tender sent through the European Communities Procurement Directives methodology was issued using the official notices in the *Official Journal* of the European Communities. Much of the original specification was still valid but a new section explained what was required as the on-screen version of the test system.

In terms of getting the new system up and running it was important to research the usability of such a system to members of the public and for the purposes of testing. The approach was very different to the existing one and some of the test questions would not as easily be adapted to screen performance. The test content is reviewed every year when the question bank is updated and poor or no longer relevant questions are removed. For the purposes of ensuring adequate coverage of the Highway Code material a new core subject category was introduced. The use of computer screens to conduct tests needed to be managed from many different aspects much more pertinent than previously. The effects of using screens instead of a written approach had to be assessed in terms of visualisation versus duration of the test. Lighting and possible emissions from the computer would be a concern which previously might not have been such an important issue. During the development of the specification there was much deliberation as to whether to opt for a touch-screen version which meant that the candidates sitting the test only needed to understand what the screen requirements were, or to opt for a push-button approach that might require more knowledge and understanding of computer technology.

The DSA needed to ensure both for members of the public and the DSA and their service providers smooth transition from the outgoing paper-based test to the new on-screen version. Focused contract and operational management ensured that the handover was run smoothly with minimum disruption to all concerned. A strategy was adopted where all aspects of the new system were subjected to rigorous user acceptance testing just as trials had been completed for the paper-based test previously. The DSA needed to be satisfied with the outcome of these tests prior to any planned implementation process. Significant benefit could be derived for the DSA with the new system in terms of reduced administrative costs of telephone queries seeking results as the test results with the on-screen version would be available at no extra cost at the end of the test. The nature of the software on the on-screen test facilitated a new computerised marking scheme that reduced the demand for re-marks. Similarly the on-screen computerised version of the test placed the answer into the box automatically once the candidate touched that box. Whilst review was possible by the candidate, there was no necessity for the candidate to be accurate with the positioning of the 'X' as in the paper-based system; this then reduced the need for manual intervention on the marking output. Management information on the nature, form and frequency etc is more readily available from the new system too. All of these developments directly affect the candidates taking the test in a positive way.

Whilst customer focus had always been important to the DSA there was an increased emphasis on the customer. These are identified as the candidates for the test; and parents of those taking the test since a high proportion of the candidates are aged between 17 and 21 and parents are more likely to be involved in the 'driving process'. There is therefore a high level of interface between the service provider and these parents and the candidate; as well as between the practical and theory test examiner and instructors and these other customers. The general road users too are customers of the DSA as the output for the DSA affects all of them. A reconsideration of the necessary performance outputs for this new generation testing system was undertaken along with a renewed examination of the specification, aesthetics etc.

On-Screen Theory Test Trials

To ensure that the new system would work effectively, a trial scheme was set up over a one-month period at five centres in Britain to demonstrate the options and make an assessment of the best approach. A company arranging the trial was required only to undertake this work; it was separate to any companies that might eventually deliver the software and/or the system. Feedback on these trials showed that the on-screen might work better from the suppliers perspective with either a computer in a kiosk or a computer on a table in a room alongside others. The touch-screen version of the test was measured for robustness against the press-button approach. The style of information used in both versions would be affected by the version chosen. Overall the cost of maintaining the touch-screen version proved less and so this was approach was chosen.

Data was provided to suppliers to enter onto the computers and was verified across the test environment. The change process from one system had to be managed effectively as there was discovered a lack of synchronisation with the planned review of the existing question bank. At one centre in Birmingham staff were sent on retraining to learn how to manage special needs under such a test environment. Similarly there was a need to ensure that questions to be used in the on-screen test were appropriate to that medium and so staff were also retrained in writing questions for the touch-screen method of presentation. In addition to this there needed to be a more detailed specification of the type of screen that was to be used and the nature of the writing on that screen from a visibility point of view. Even a choice of font size could affect the effect of the test on candidates. The DSA were conscious of the style that could be used in the screen approach and they wished to appear professional and forward thinking in their style but also have a traditional appearance that conveyed a serious business that was to be undertaken in the form of the driving theory test. Educationally the DSA understood that only so much data should appear on the screen at once so the less busy the screen looked the clearer the picture that could be conveyed to the candidate. This version as much to do with costs was static in its visual approach but plans for later upgrades of the system would incorporate moving images on-screen representing the question delivery. The designers recognised that this might cause confusion and so would incorporate a moving and stopping motion where the question was on something dangerous. The issue of how humans interface with computers was of interest to the DSA as they thought that this might have an effect on the ability to pass such a test. Psychologists were engaged to explore this matter by the DSA. This revealed certain factors that have been absorbed into the design of the screen and the images transposed to that screen in terms of colours, size of font, button image and size, etc.

Performance of the On-Screen Theory Test

The DSA have found that the new test proved to be an accurate, reliable and user-friendly testing system. Added value has been provided in the form of results and feedback on success in the tests can be given in 30 minutes, at no extra costs. Important design criteria lie in the added assistance that the test provides for special needs candidates with improved multimedia features such as spoken tests in English. These features specifically aid those candidates with dyslexia and other reading difficulties. The tests can also be listened to in 15 languages. A video in sign language is available for the hearing-impaired. With the advent of the new on-screen approach to the test, candidates can prepare for sitting the test by loading a CD-ROM into an available computer to practice the approach that they will need to take to complete it. At first the CD-ROM contained 1000 questions and answers in the bank of car and motorcycle tests. There was a training disc and a practical test that used the same screen design as the actual test.

Role of the Procurement in the Organisation

The DSA as an organisation see their procurement function as a strategic function effecting the development and funding potential for the entire business. This particular contract area involved complex issues of design law, financial aspects and negotiations based on delivery and performance. The fact that there were actually two separate but interrelated contract specifications made this procurement a special strategic project. The procurement function worked with other internal functions as a team and also interfaced with external customers and stakeholders in the process. Much time had to be invested to ensure that this contract was 'right' and as such had senior management commitment to the leading role that the procurement function was taking throughout. The process had to be in place to allow the procurement function to act. A high level of personal commitment and ownership of the procurement project was expected and given from all involved across the DSA.

Conclusions

This case study looked at the development of the Driving Theory Test, at the Driving Standards Agency (DSA). The driving test in Great Britain now consists of a separate theory and practical driving test, for which the DSA are responsible. The DSA began the development of this theory test contract and in 1996 a transition period for its introduction was initiated. The test has progressed from a written test in 1996 to a touch-screen theory test in January 2000. This research tracked the development of this very complex design-rich theory test contract and explains the best practice process that was utilised by the DSA in the development of the end product– the two-part driving test.

The case study shows how the product and service represented here was researched and developed from a written-based test to a computerised test. Many stakeholders were involved in the process and much psychology had to be introduced into the design of the visual approach of the product. Various circumstances surrounding the use of on-screen technology coupled with the development of appropriate test questions had to be taken into account. This meant that the DSA had to engage with educationalists, psychologists, computer software engineers, technicians, service delivery providers, and various equipment manufacturers along with users of the test facilities, the law, and the European Union in the course of the development of the entire contract provision.

The aims of the DSA have been cited previously but it is clear that the nature of this contract puts it at the very heart of the DSA business. Apart from the more perhaps obvious implications of incorrect purchase of electronic testing equipment or a less effective service delivery mechanism behind the test delivery for the candidates taking the test and the general public using the roads in Britain, this highly effective and successful contract represented a 25% increase in turnover for the DSA. If the business of driving tests fails then no tests can be held and no new drivers can obtain licences as the practical test depends on this theory test. On the wider scale failure in this area can affect jobs and numbers of employees in the industry. The DSA also made strong links between road safety and the overall economy of the country.

As a result of substantial experience developed on this contract the DSA in Great Britain has been invited to provide consultancy to the Ireland Agency to assist them in developing a similar test facility.

Lessons Learnt

This contract represented a major project over a number of years for the DSA. It is testament to the commitment of the procurement team and the management of the DSA organisation as a whole in terms of design thinking, incorporation of stakeholders in the process and the overall financial success that the contract represents to the DSA. The DSA have been open in their discussions of this work and have offered several lessons learnt by them in the course of the contract development work since 1994 through to 2000.

- There is much benefit to be derived from a dedicated team for such a complex and strategically critical procurement.
- Where there is a requirement for such specialised knowledge development a plan to gain that knowledge and the development of strong links with people that know must be made.
- The project was in effect running over a six-year period. There is a

proven need for continuity of the team for the duration of the project, for without it much valuable knowledge and time can be lost.

- The choice of personnel is important for a procurement project of this nature and the ability to develop research strength in the team is vital.

- Customer focus is of paramount importance. The entire concept of theory tests separate to the practical driving test was new in 1994. Quantum leaps in terms of development of those tests and then the computerisation of them were made over the contract period. Keeping an eye to the customer throughout ensures that the product will remain realistic in terms of its usability, acceptability and delivery in its market, ie the driving world in Great Britain.

- A steady and feet-on-the-ground approach to the development of the computerisation of the already developed written test was highly recommended. A strategy for that development involving many other individuals alongside procurement staff has proven to greatly aid the success of the entire process.

- Remember to always ask the 'why' question throughout the development of the contract, the product and the service. Determining why an aspect needs to be like it is or determining why it should be like it is assures that the product that is developed is grounded in reality.

- The more critical the project or procurement area, the more an organisation should move to higher levels of involvement of suppliers. A partnership style arrangement should be sought so as to gain from both parties' experience and the determination of the requirements for the work.

- The DSA became reliant upon the service provider for such a business-critical contract that the 'right' supplier and the 'right' relationship had to be developed.

- So much of this procurement delivery relies on service providers to deliver effectively that there need to be clearly laid out parameters on expected performance of the product and the service from the suppliers in the contract.

- Good communications with suppliers are required so that regular meetings on a weekly, monthly, and at quarterly periods with senior personnel should be set up to discuss the overall performance and responsibility for the delivery of the contract. A joint strategy for the development and maintenance of relationships, service delivery and performance should be developed between parties in the contract.

- The value of staff development and training in the development of the computerised system and the test questions is immense. A clear understanding of the process itself and of how candidates might react to the new system aids the development of specifications for and with suppliers. It also sets the scene for appropriate service provision to provide a backdrop to the test delivery experience.

- The role of trials and testing the system prior to implementation proved worthwhile in terms of attuning the actual delivery to the expected one in terms of performance.

- Time is a commodity that is expensive to utilise but more expensive if it is not utilised effectively. The DSA felt that if it were to do the job over again that much more time devoted to the evaluation of the options on the software development would be required.

- That everything has a price was learnt in the course of the contract; this proved to be an expensive lesson. Many variations had to be introduced into the service delivery contract to ensure that the contract delivery ran smoothly. It was felt that it was difficult to determine some of these requirements prior to the contract development as a new outsourced service delivery was adopted. However, had some of the variations been incorporated prior to the contract award these would have worked out to be less expensive then to add them afterwards.

- The most important lesson to learn was to always remember the purpose of the exercise, in this case to provide a product and service to improve road safety as a legal requirement from Europe.

Specific Questions

1. Consider the development of the theory test from 1994 through 2000 in terms of procurement process and design issues by tracking the number and nature of issues that had to be incorporated into the overall project.

2. Discuss the importance of the early inclusion of these issues to the success of the entire project.

3. Consider the DSA study in the light of the Pugh Model of Design Boundaries to determine how many of the cited 'design' and 'procurement' criteria were considered in the development of these ICT and the service delivery contracts.

4. Identify the stakeholders, their involvement and explain what impact their non-involvement might have had on the success of the project.

Chapter 6
Driver and Vehicle Licensing Agency Case Study

Introduction

This case study looks at the procurement process undertaken for the development of the contract for the Vehicle Excise Duty Discs that are issued to provide a road usage licence to vehicles on the British roads, issued by the Driver and Vehicle Licensing Agency (DVLA) on behalf of government. This contract is a core activity for the Agency, as it provides the visual display mechanism, in vehicles, of road drivers' compliance with the road traffic and taxation laws in Great Britain. This contract therefore has a very high profile for the Agency and design is of paramount importance in the development process.

The DVLA was established as an executive agency in April 1990 and is now one of the Driver, Vehicle, and Operator (DVO) organisations in the Department of the Environment, Transport and the Regions (DETR).

The aim of this Agency is to facilitate road safety and general law enforcement by maintaining registers of drivers and vehicles and the collection of government taxation in the form of Vehicle Excise Duty (VED). The tax is collected by the DVLA, for the government, through the sale of Vehicle Excise Duty Discs (VEDD) that must be displayed on the windscreen of each vehicle using the roads in Britain.

The focus of our case study is the development and procurement of VEDD. However, other key tasks of the DVLA are to record amendments to driver and vehicle details to meet the needs of law enforcement agencies. The DVLA also issue and withdraw drivers' licences and issue registration documents and annual licences to vehicle keepers. These aspects of the DVLA's work are pertinent to the production, development and management of the VEDD as the reason that a vehicle on the road carries a registration plate is so that, through the record, the number on that plate uniquely identifies the particular vehicle, and then this identifies a particular person responsible for that vehicle. The DVLA issues documents to individuals concerned, which form their record of that linkage. An official record is kept of the driving entitlements of all drivers and the DVLA issues driving licences based on that record. The VEDD plays a key role in the fulfilment of these key tasks, as it aids the maintenance of registers and the collection of taxation from members of the public and businesses who use the roads. The VEDD because of its important legal status also provides the opportunity to keep many links with other aspects of driving a car, for example, links to both insurance and vehicle MOT.

The DVLA has a wide customer base, serving motorists and members of the general public both directly and indirectly. It serves Treasury, police, the courts, local authorities, commercial companies and their trade associations. All are important, and the DVLA has a strategic commitment to good customer service. The DVLA examined in this research has only driver responsibilities for Great Britain. Driver licensing in Northern Ireland is covered by a separate agency, DVLANI, responsible to the Department of Environment for Northern Ireland.

The design of VEDD is of vital importance, as it must provide the facility to record as a minimum all vehicles' registrations and their make and model details. There is a facility to record and hold data on the cost of and payment for, the vehicle licence disc, its expiry date and therefore it provides much needed information for law enforcement in this area of vehicle ownership, usage and legality.

The requirement on members of the public to purchase and display VEDD sets up the need for the DVLA to provide purchase services with various other businesses and agencies. VEDD are sold to members of the public mainly at the Post Office, but more recently to fleet car operators and new car dealers who have the facility to sell licences on their premises. This transpired as main car dealers wanted a role in electing a process for authorisation and distribution of the discs as they had a vested interest in the length of time it would take to obtain discs for new vehicles.

The police too have a vested interest in the design of the discs. Consequently, there is a special police unit set up to liaise with the DVLA enforcement section, known as the blue liaison unit, specifically to tackle changes or identify and solve any problems with the discs to help with law enforcement.

The History Behind the Vehicle Excise Duty Disc

The concept for this VEDD was developed some 30 years ago to provide evidence for the payment of vehicle excise duty to the government for a specific period of time. There also needed to be a way of making a comparison on specific licence VEDD with a specific car so as to associate one vehicle with one driver/owner. The concept too incorporated a link with the roadworthiness of the vehicle and its insurance.

Legality of the Disc

The VEDD is a legal document that is required to be purchased and displayed by all vehicle owners, under the Vehicle Excise Registration Act 1994. A vehicle cannot be legally driven on the roads without a valid VEDD. Apart from the government using VEDD as a method of tax collection it is mostly the police, to ensure validity of the vehicle, who use VEDD. Similarly when a vehicle undergoes its Motor Operation Test (MOT) the garage conducting the test is required by law to make a check upon the VEDD to establish the validity of the vehicle. Similarly, when a VEDD is purchased a link is made to the vehicle's insurance and to a valid driving licence, so that if neither valid insurance nor driver licence is held for the vehicle or the driver, then no VEDD will be issued. Thus the law stretches it boundaries across roadworthiness, lawful use of the highway and ensures that redress in terms of some form of insurance cover is available for other road users in the event of a road traffic accident.

The DVLA needed to set up a contract, therefore, that there would be adequate supply of discs to all sales outlets in the public domain and within the motor trade. Ultimately, prolonged failure to supply the appropriate number of VEDD would have many repercussions for society as well as individuals in that society. Throughout Great Britain the main Post Office Supply Depot at Hemel Hempstead supplies 4000 post offices. A vehicle registration network supplies a further 40 offices with discs and other franchised dealers through an automated first registration and licensing system known as an AFRL system. Some attempt has been made to streamline the process from Vehicle Registration Offices to the main car dealers to effect more control over distribution through this system. Individuals can purchase a VEDD to cover the licensed road use for a period of either six or twelve months. This puts extra burden on the production, delivery and distribution of the VEDD throughout Great Britain. Figure X shows the distribution network in Great Britain.

The entire process of development and distribution costs £700K per annum. Some 60 million individual licences in books of 20 are produced for use throughout the United Kingdom. The production of VEDD must be in a continuous format so as to keep track of the issue of these discs to fleet operators, etc.

Whilst the DVLA (GB) has only responsibility to supply Great Britain they have close links with Northern Ireland and their issue sequences, etc. The normal VEDD is referenced under the code of V300 and some one hundred thousand are produced each year for Great Britain alone; eight hundred thousand per annum are produced for Northern Ireland. A Heavy Goods Vehicle Licence is referenced under the code V2999 and only 8000 of these are produced per annum.

One of the main challenges for both the DVLA in Northern Ireland and in Great Britain is the estimation of the need for VEDD. Forecasting can be very difficult due to changing government policy in respect of car driving and licensing costs, etc. Such was the discrepancy in estimation in 1998 that there was approximately 60% wastage in Northern Ireland. There is a fine balance to be struck in the estimation of the production requirement for VEDD to cover need throughout the country and ensuring that all outlets have sufficient quantity of VEDD in time. Delay in delivery of VEDD to outlets can have significant impact on government revenue and members of the publics' ability to drive their vehicles within the legal framework laid down in Great Britain.

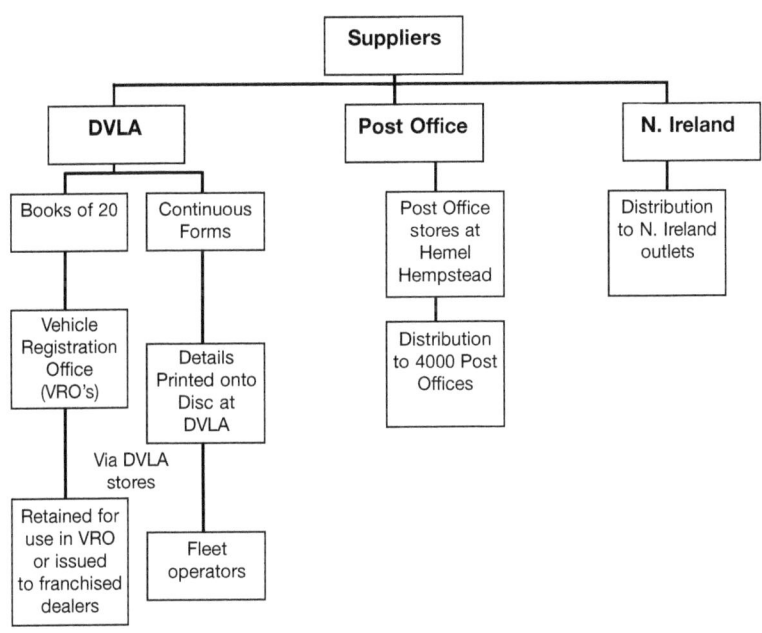

Figure 1: Network distribution of Vehicle Licence Discs in Great Britain

Competition for Sources of Supply

VEDD were the subject of sole sourcing until 1998 when a decision was taken by DVLA to dual-source so that back up quantities of the disc could be obtained in the event of breakdown in supply. There was recognition, at this time, of poor contract management within DVLA and the original contractor appeared to hold back from divulging commercial and technical information, pertinent to the production of VEDD, from DVLA. This data was not held by DVLA and thus the matter became particularly important after the decision to dual-source was taken, as such information was required to provide details to any new company who would be engaged in the development of VEDD in the future.

Despite having developed the specification initially with one supplier the agency operated under the European Procurement Regulations, which necessitated the use of competitive tender for all procurements of this nature. In addition, the monies involved in the contract required the DVLA to issue a European tender to invite potential suppliers to bid for the contract. A decision was taken at DVLA that the tender should be run on a restricted basis that thus reduced the number of tenderers who would be invited to bid for the work. As the agency was operating within the confines of government regulation it was limited in its ability to become involved in commercial activity with suppliers. It was seen that potential to gain commercial advantage with the sale of VEDD existed but this could not therefore be taken up by DVLA. There was, however, recognition that the dual-sourcing issue would have a bearing on the outcome of the tender and the numbers invited would need to match the potential to operate with two contractors.

Contract Development Process

In the event six potential suppliers where invited to bid, using a full tender documentation process. A full specification had been drawn up for the production, development and the management of the contract. This will be discussed later. During the evaluation process records of any amendments that were required either by the tenderers or by DVLA to the production planning were kept. A process of contract management too was set out in the original tender documentation but clarified during the contract set up stage and this process is documented throughout the run of the contract period. In addition to this there was a requirement to establish a quarterly meeting process, laid down within the tender documentation, between each of the suppliers and the DVLA. As many of the earlier difficulties had arisen in the lack of communication and the failure to develop a sound relationship between the supplier and DVLA, the new contract was to be based upon a closer working relationship where any outstanding issues or problems that arose between the quarterly meetings could be resolved. To facilitate this there was a plan of monitoring of sequences in the process of production, delivery and distribution all of which formed documentation to support the existing process and to provide material to learn from on renewing the contract at the end of its term. During the contract it was planned that performance measure levels should be mapped on graphs displaying issues like production output levels on time, service levels, security breaches and delivery, etc. This data would be shared with the suppliers so as to improve communication and improve the entire contractual experience for all parties concerned.

Environmental Considerations

DVLA had to take cognisance of the environmental circumstances in which they worked. The design of VEDD rested with the DVLA under Patent, so this affected the nature of the contract specification. The DVLA had to recognise their intellectual property in the contract but also seek to liaise with suppliers on the production and management of distribution, etc for the contract. The nature of the contract and its specification was restricted by the extent of the government legislation surrounding the purpose of the production of VEDD. The impact upon the level of contract work involved can be affected by individual members of the public and business response to the government levy on road usage. Each year, there has been a tendency to increase the overall levy of taxation on road users through this VEDD. There has also been significant pressure to reduce usage of the roads by increasing the cost of fuel for use in vehicles. This will affect the way vehicles are used on the road but also will have an impact upon the number of new cars that might be bought due to the cost of running them. Similarly, in an effort to save the environment there has been pressure to reduce the level of pollution exuded by vehicles, through offering a reduced VED levy for lower vehicle engine sizes. This environmental factor too will affect the number and nature of the requirement of VEDD over an annual period. There may ultimately be a reduction in the number of new vehicles and thereby new VEDD needed but this environment may affect the number of six-monthly VEDD as opposed to twelve-monthly ones as members of the public may eek out their payment of the levy over a longer period. Environmental protection of renewable sources such as paper may have an effect on the way that the DVLA seek to have VEDD produced. Recycled paper has been used in many industries; potential for such use of this paper in these circumstances may need to be considered in more detail in future production of VEDD.

As the contract for VEDD has developed so political and ethical issues have come to the fore and have exposed a need to change the manufacture of VEDD in aesthetic ways. The contract was set in such a way as to permit such changes that became necessary for technical or other important reasons. The development of the VEDD constantly undergoes review. Redesign of the VEDD itself has been required to take account of for example the legal requirement to produce all documents in Welsh and English. The VEDD needed to be bilingual. This change had quite a significant impact on the size and detailed design, as the languages are totally different in construction. Similarly, specific colours used on the face of VEDD can trigger societal issues, for instance the colours orange and green, red and blue in N. Ireland can be controversial and so are therefore the subject of discussion for the production process for VEDD. As a result political factors of all kinds can have a strong impact upon the contract performance.

Market Constraints

There were also significant market restraints upon the contract for VEDD production. Security was a key factor in the entire process. Given that the VEDD was not only designed for the purpose of collecting government tax but also served to demonstrate the current status of the vehicle and its driver in terms of legality to use the road by the individual responsible for it, there was a high risk that counterfeit VEDD would be attractive to members of the public who either could or would not pay the tax and for those who had had legal restrictions placed on driving a vehicle. Repercussions of counterfeit VEDD in operation would be an obvious reduction in government revenue but would also permit individuals, for whom the courts had cause to restrict or ban their legal use of the road, to continue driving. These individuals could cause further danger to other road users and if they were proved to be the cause of an accident for instance then they would not have the legal cover in terms of insurance to pay for the rectification of the damage to people or vehicles. To this end prevention and detection of forgery and counterfeit of the licence is a high priority for the DVLA and consequently one of their main roles. The VEDD, and even the lack of the display of it in the windscreen of the vehicle, is the source of information to establish for example evidence of an individual who has been banned from driving a vehicle with no insurance, or that a vehicle is stolen. Therefore the contract for VEDD had to reflect this important security aspect in terms of both the choice of supplier and their technical capability in the production of VEDD. This VEDD is a very individual product; it is clear that issues such as the method of production, standards of printing, secure transportation and distribution and storage facilities, etc are important. There would be few suppliers in the market place that could undertake such a complex contract.

The European tender exercise led to the award of a new contract in 1998 with two suppliers, for a period of three years with the opportunity to extend the contract for a further two years. The contract was awarded to the original supplier in the UK and to a new supplier based in mainland Europe. There were many stakeholders involved in the process of selection of the suppliers and the product and services that would be offered under the contract. Engineering personnel were involved in decision making pertinent to the design features of the product itself. Other participants involved were members of an internal DVLA policy vehicle group, the police liaison group, local DVLA office network groups and members of the finance function within DVLA.

Once the new contract was awarded there were significant teething problems in running the new contract, as DVLA had some difficulties in persuading the original company to share information on the production and design features of the VEDD. Naturally, the original supplier was reluctant to loose the sole supplier status, despite issues that had been discussed with them on the levels of delivery of the service. There was no blame attached to the original supplier, as much of the information held by them was of an experiential nature that was not easily transferred to others either in DVLA or at the new contractors.

Vehicle Excise Duty Disc Specification

The detailed specification for the original design had been compiled within the DVLA and after the initial difficulties were resolved the new suppliers worked with the original suppliers to develop a more detailed requirement that is still in use.

Characteristics of Disc Design

The DVLA sought innovative ideas from the new tendered companies as to the best method of production of VEDD. The specification itself was very detailed in its nature and required significant levels of design speciality. The product is protected by patent and so this dictates many of the design characteristics of VEDD.

Security Considerations

Specific detail on the weight and quality of VEDD is included to provide a basis of design characteristics for the purposes of security. The weight and the quality of the paper are important also in respect of the standard period of exposure for the product. As a VEDD is displayed on the windscreen of each vehicle it must be capable of withstanding the elements such as sunlight for a period of up to 12 months. Similarly, many of the design features are incorporated to provide the maximum level of security for the VEDD. This means that there is a requirement to undertake significant tests on the design to ensure that the VEDD are unable to be copied. A key to such protection is an in-built design feature in the paper and coloured ink utilised in the manufacture of the VEDD. A specific quality of paper upon which the VEDD is to be printed using the chosen photogravure method of production is described. Adding to the design features for security purposes, the VEDD have ink inserted in the recesses of the paper using deeper colour, which also aims to stop the ability to copy the VEDD, by those who might wish to defraud the government. This method of design is a less common way to produce the VEDD but it is deemed a more effective method to ensure security, as there is less opportunity for counterfeit when it is used.

The use of special ink in an anti-photo feature, that now incorporates a FADE chemical too, adds to the level of the security of the VEDD. This chemical acts when the disc is copied so that the colour will fade, thus invalidating the disc. Under normal circumstances the ink is light fast. The back of disc contains a bleeding ink to stop any change of details on the front of the disc.

Figure 2

Central to the design of VEDD is the development of serial numbers that proved to be a predominant feature of the issue of the disc and are used by car dealers, the police, the Post Office, as well as the DVLA. Due to this predominance the design included a space for expiry dates designed in large bold type, with the top blackened so as to offer the feature for police validity that is easily seen at a distance from the vehicle. This addition had a big effect on the print process and particularly the ink setting process that had to be adapted to capture this feature. The serial number on the VEDD of course links the legality of the vehicle to drive on the roads to the issue for a particular vehicle and so is traceable back if the registration of the owner or registered driver of the vehicle changes. The Post Office has to be issued with a security pen for writing on VEDD again to minimise the likelihood of alteration of details written on VEDD by the authorised personnel. This meant that a requirement to train Post Office staff in writing on the discs had to be undertaken as the disc production process is very specific and failure to write in the appropriate spaces could invalidate the disc. Any changes to the specification of VEDD can lead to a change in the production machinery and other machines such as cutters, involved in the development of VEDD. Due to changes in the expiry date aspect of the design there needed to be precise calibration on machines to process VEDD. The changes to the machinery had to be negotiated with the maker of the machine.

Even the size, style, number and dimension of the perforations round the sides of the disc became a security feature. This was clever use of design criterion, as the perforations appeared initially to be a way of separating the disc from its surrounds in order to fit into the holder on the windscreen.

Size Versus Visibility of the Disc

The precise size of VEDD had to be considered carefully as VEDD must be positioned in the vehicle windscreen of all vehicles. The size of VEDD needed to ensure that discs could be easily seen by many key enforcement officers such as the police and traffic wardens, who used it as a tool for discerning other pertinent facts about the car and its owner, but that it was not so large that it could be the source of accidents through blocking the view of the driver nor distracting attention from the road. As the VEDD developed, the data content for VEDD became quite precise and this too dictated the size of the disc as it could only be reduced in size so far before illegible print started to appear. Another consideration too for the dimensions of the disc lay in the packaging of VEDD for transportation and distribution. There were a high proportion of discs both being produced and transported across the country. This constituted a high cost that could be cut down through better consideration of the weight and size of the VEDD. These issues were taken into account with the other factors pertaining to size in the early design.

Contract Costs

The overall cost of the product, ie the VEDD, is of course important but it is the security and size characteristics that are predominant. The price of the production process and the costs associated with the contract are established in the tendering process. There is no breakdown into overhead costs however. Value for Money remains the key principle upon which the contract is let. Cost reduction, prior to and once the contract is let, revolves around the need to cut down on the cost of attributed services for the backup of the product itself.

Significant government revenue is attributable to the sale of VEDD and this plays a part in the contract management and support features on the contract. To this end a series of schedules on production and delivery and costs associated with this are required from the supplier. Payment to the supplier is dependent upon delivery of VEDD on time to the various locations in good quality and in the right quantity. However, the monies raised by the sale of VEDD at Post Offices, VRO's and car dealerships needs to be controlled and collected. There is a strong relationship between the VEDD issued to each retail outlet and the revenue expected from them.

Detailed records need to be kept and passed to the DVLA about the throughput for VEDD and those not sold recorded for return, etc.

The DVLA are responsible for payment to the suppliers for their role on the contract and the collection of revenue from the various outlets involved under the contract too.

Customer

Many customers have been identified in the course of the development of the case study. Whilst the principle end customers are members of the public and the car trade who purchase VEDD from the DVLA, they are only doing so through enforcement of law. The nature of the VEDD and the design characteristics are not directly discussed with them. Thought has been put into how VEDD are issued to end customers and ease of use features, for example books of 20 discs are printed for Post Offices so as to more easily track issue and sequence numbers for the public. Guidance notes explaining how to display, what the licence entitles individuals to do, etc, have also been developed for end customers and these are issued accompanying VEDD issued from central DVLA offices. Those bodies and official enforcers of the road traffic legislation (such as the police) who effect design changes in terms of visibility and data content, etc have been consulted. The various Vehicle Registration Offices too have had a significant input into the development of the VEDD and accompanying machinery to support its distribution to the public.

Timescale for Product Development and Delivery

The production schedule for VEDD is divided between the two suppliers in the contract. Further separation occurs in the production run for those discs expiring in twelve months and those to expire in six months. The VEDD for 2001 have been produced one year and six months in advance of the date of requirement. The VEDD design production is complete in August 2000 to facilitate print requirements and delivery for January 2001. The contract manager confirmed the print run to the printer in July 2000, in terms of volumes of the licences for certain expiry dates. There is also a check made at that time with the Post Office, DVLA historical evidence, fleet licences, N. Ireland requirements, etc to coordinate volumes and then to decide on the serial numbers to be used for that particular print run. An instruction is given on the printing, finishing and package characteristics that are required for it. Three months after manufacture the VEDD are delivered to DVLA security stores or are held at the supplier's warehouse. At each stage of production output is monitored and a staggered schedule of delivery is established. Three months prior to sale to the public and trade VEDD are dispensed to the various points of sale, such as the Post Office. Consequently there is a need for strong links between DVLA and the suppliers on the delivery sequencing, as VEDD are renewable at the end of each month throughout the year. A massive security system swings into operation of the delivery of VEDD to all establishments including security cameras, sealed vaults, security cages and revolving the storage batches.

Quantities of VEDD required have been mentioned already but this factor has a significant impact on the delivery cycle. The quantities and delivery scheduling are based upon historical evidence, however following trends has not proved important in the management of the delivery of the VEDD. The VEDD are sent to DVLA with a sequenced number for security. There needs to be a recorded link between the money taken at the various distribution outlets and the revenue that they will bring to the government through the DVLA. This puts an increased emphasis on not only the volume of VEDD produced but on the distribution of these to outlets where the revenue is collected from their sale.

Production Sampling

As there are many security features in the VEDD production process and each must be in place correctly, there is an established need to sample test VEDD for colour and ink penetration. Similarly the significance of the production schedule for expiry dates for VEDD is regularly scanned through the sample process. The new contract built in quality assurance methods to the production process and management of the contract to try to reduce the level of sample testing that might need to be undertaken by the DVLA. As a consequence there are laboratories available at each supplier to ensure that the various processes have been applied properly throughout the sequence of production. If any fault is detected in the developed sample then the entire batch must go back to the production company for re-test and a prompt reply is required to ensure the fault is rectified for future production. The faulty batch(es) must be destroyed.

Disposal

As security for the entire production, delivery and distribution process has been a central focus for the DVLA, the disposal of VEDD requires equal attention. A system is in place whereby two people need to be present for the disposal of VEDD after their expiry date. Those VEDD that have not been issued and are surplus to requirement after the expiry date are returned to the supplier from, for instance, the Post Office for secure disposal. A system of full accountability and a comparable reward system are in operation with the supplier for the production and disposal of VEDD.

Role of the Procurement in the Organisation

The procurement function has played a major role in the development of this contract which itself has a major impact upon the performance of the DVLA as a whole. The procurement function within the DVLA is involved in strategically important procurement decisions and as such should have a central role for the organisation. However, the procurement personnel felt that they are not recognised for the important role that they play or the impact that could be made by the function on reduction of costs and savings for the DVLA as a whole. They felt that this was because they have not been identified as a significant part of the strategic management team within the agency. As in other departments in the public sector the procurement team are tied with the finance department. The level of recognition for the team within the organisation lies around the tactical or business unit level of the organisation rather than at the strategic level. The more the procurement team works to achieve savings and reductions and can effect the performance of the DVLA such as in the VEDD contract the more likely it is to rise in esteem within the organisation. The DVLA have set up a commercial director to manage opportunities to develop monies for the DVLA, such as contract is the sale of personalised number plates. There too is a strong link to the main Department of the Environment, Transport and the Regions (DETR) who have a more strategic view of the role of procurement. Staff in both the DETR and in the DVLA have been encouraged to undertake professional qualifications in the field of Purchasing and Supply Management.

Conclusions

The subject of this case study has quite an impact on government revenue in respect of taxation for road usage in Great Britain. This case study has been examined as a sound approach to one specific public sector procurement contract that required sophisticated design criterion; an understanding of governmental policy and legislation on road usage and taxation; high levels of co-ordination of various law enforcement bodies; regulation, monitoring and control of the product, the funds; and the distribution and delivery schedules designed specifically for the purpose of production, movement and sale of VEDD of behalf of the government.

The repercussions of failure of such a contract could have a significant effect on many different individuals and agencies in terms of legal use of the roads in Great Britain.

Lessons Learnt

This contract for the DVLA was of paramount importance to their ability to meet the aims and objectives of the DVLA. To this end they learnt several lessons in the development of the design of the VEDD itself and the supporting features for that contract.

- There was a need to hold the intellectual property rights on their key product within the DVLA and not to allow it to be held in the hands of the only original supplier of VEDD known to the organisation.
- The understanding of the importance of design was enhanced for the DVLA on this contract as many of the requirements for security, clarity of print and the method of recording data on such a small circumference were innovatively resolved by considering design early and in the context of the totality of the product.
- Design features are important not only in the development of the product but in the supporting equipment and the service too. The nature of storage, delivery and distribution of the VEDD product, throughout Great Britain, was sophisticated and warranted significant design focus and should be seen as important as the design of the product itself.
- The need for securely held documentation on the development of the VEDD was very important.
- Contract management for the DVLA had to be improved and through breakdown in communication on that contract management much angst was experienced when they wished to make changes to the contract procedure and production processes in respect of the key product for their agency.
- The DVLA learnt the importance of buyer/supplier relationships that had to be improved during the course of the development of the new

contract tender documentation and afterward at the start of the new contract term. Despite the competitive mechanism for developing contractual relationships at the start of the process DVLA found that time and effort spent getting to know the supplier and working with them, during the contract, paid dividends when issues arose that needed to be resolved quickly and effectively.

- The need for design features to be understood and to be permeated throughout the supply chain was recognised as many stakeholders across the process such as the police, the Post Office and the VRO needed to have an input into the design, distribution and control of VEDD for the DVLA and the government too, if the entire process was to be effective and efficient and successfully managed in terms of design.

- Communication is a key factor to be managed throughout the process. Noticeably, at points in the process where problems arose such as time slippage of production or delivery, good communications aided resolution of the matter and helped to put contingency plans into practice.

- The implications for failure on this contract could be devastating. Counterfeits, wastage and errors on VEDD were the main concerns during the development of the VEDD design and through the contract management. Considering these at the start and maintaining a focus upon them throughout the constant design review cycles helped to minimise the likelihood and actual occurrences of the problem areas.

Case Synopsis

This case study has been developed with the help of the procurement team at the DVLA based in Swansea in S. Wales. The case study examined the development of the contract for the Vehicle Excise Duty Discs (VEDD) that by law must be purchased either bi-annually or annually and displayed by all vehicle owners in Great Britain as a method of collection of government tax to pay for the use of roads. This contract for VEDD is a core activity for the Agency, as it provided the visual display mechanism, in vehicles, of road drivers' compliance with the road traffic and taxation laws in Great Britain. This contract therefore has a very high profile for the Agency and design is of paramount importance in the developmental process. This particular contract exercise is still being effectively managed through its third year. The study beigins with an explanation of the aims of the DVLA itself and follows the progress of the design of the specification and the support chain behind it. The case study begins with the procurement team about to begin the European tendering process. A dual-sourced approach is taken to permit backup for the supply of the VEDD because of the importance of the contract product and to signify the criticality of supply of these VEDD to the Agency and the government too. The design of the disc is duscussed revealing that the most important factors lie with the security of the development of the discs so as to avoid as much as possible fraud or counterfeit. There are many stakeholders involved in the process ranging from the police and traffic wardens to the Post Office and Vehicle Registration Offices through to the end customer members of the British public. A strong reliance rests upon the suppliers' elements to the contract such as the design, paper, ink dye, printing, storage, transportation and distribution.

The contract has been managed well and the DVLA are rightly proud of the progress that has been made with the contract. They have been open about the lessons learnt and where they sought to improve the contract from the earlier sole-sourced model previously used for the procurement of the VEDD.

Teaching and Learning Objectives
- To provide students with the opportunity to understand a case relaying best practice in the public sector procurement arena that

explicitly incorporates design concepts early in its procurement strategy.
- To provide students with the basis for a discussion on the procurement path taken and the importance of design to both the product, service and the supply chain behind it all.
- To help students understand areas of synergy between design criteria for the development of new products and the procurement criteria for the development of sound procurement decisions.
- To provide scope to analyse the design issues considered in the development of a vehicle licence contract.
- To examine the effect of design on procurement strategies.
- To explore the importance of involving key stakeholders in the procurement process throughout.

Main Issues Raised

- Consideration of design concepts
- Consideration of the impact of design upon the identification of need
- Consideration of design upon the finished procurement contract
- Consideration of procurement decision criteria
- Consideration of key elements of strategic procurement
- Consideration of the importance of external and internal interface in the development of the requirement for procurement
- Consideration of the impact of organisational values, mission and culture upon procurement decisions
- Consideration of supplier/buyer relationships
- Consideration of issues such as intellectual property rights and legal factors in the development of procurement contract.

Specific Questions

1. Consider the DVLA Vehicle Excise Duty Disc case study in the light of strategic procurement planning and how design has featured in that planning.

2. Pugh's Model of Design Boundaries provided in the introduction to this book, cited 'design' and 'procurement' criteria that should be considered in the development of new products. Consider how important the inclusion of these criteria is to the success of the entire project.

3. Identify the involvement of the various stakeholders in this case study process and explain the role that they played in the development of final framework.

4. Draw a flow diagram to show the stages of involvement of these stakeholders through the development of the framework process.

The Approach Taken

The case was approached from the perspective of design issues and how the have been integrated into the procurement strategy of this contract with DVLA. The full approach in terms of questioning and method has been incorporated into the chapter of introduction in this text. The Pugh Model of Design Boundaries has been used to identify the main elements considered in new product design and those most pertinent to criteria for making decisions for various procurements throughout both the private and public sectors. This model was described at the outset of the interview for the collection of data for this case study. It was also discussed throughout the case study research to help identify the extent to which the design and procurement factors mesh together in the development of a new product where the innovation of suppliers is required to ensure that the end product is suitable for the purpose designated for it.

Chapter 7
Local Authority Procurement of Waste Management

Introduction

This case study identifies issues for consideration in the design of future contracts for the procurement of cleaning services for the purpose of waste management on local authority streets and domestic homes in the council area of East Abbeyworth in England. The case is put forward as a design and 'environmentally friendly' approach to the procurement of cleaning services. Students are invited to identify the design issues and comment upon how they might be addressed and on how they could impact the development of the service design to ensure that the council concerned meets all of the responsibilities. The approach to this matter follows an initiative across all county councils to ensure that the development of such contracts remains within government guidelines for the environmental procurement of materials and services pertinent to the cleaning services task. Waste management issues occupy a prominent place in the council business. Rather than mapping the development of the contract approach taken by this council the study develops areas for consideration in the design of services to meet the varied need that the entire waste disposal issue throws up for the council.

The case study does not examine one specific contract but rather looks at the topic of cleaning services and how designing such services is important with early consideration of design criteria to ensure that they meet both environmental and social responsibilities for the members of the public within the studied borough. These issues are equally as pertinent for any other city council and so the case could be cited in any region of Great Britain or Northern Ireland.

The City Council examined is divided into departments; the one focused upon here is that of the Health and Environmental Services Department (HESD). Its aim is to protect and promote the health, safety, and wellbeing of all who live in the borough or who come into the borough each day to work or visit. The Department is committed to providing associated services with economy and efficiency, to maximise the beneficial effect and the quality of the service. They are committed to the council-wide adoption of the corporate policy involving 'best value', which was introduced by central government for local authorities in 1998. This necessitates a series of rigorous reviews of all services and activities over a five-year period. Each county council was required by government to develop a sustainable development strategy. The strategy had to deliver the council's corporate objectives by ensuring that all of its own services, policies and programmes adhered to environmentally positive principles and that the long-term implications of decisions are adequately considered. The council is working hard to introduce environmental best practice and equipping themselves to conduct environmental audits. The development of these strategies on the environment and 'best value' fell in the regard of our subject matter to the HESD.

There are four service areas designated within the HESD department: building control; consumer protection; health protection and waste management. The range of services is diverse, however they are all operating to provide safety and health by managing and improving the physical environment of the population of the immediate borough or its transient members. The HESD has over 1000 employees servicing both internal and external customers. External services include buildings contracts, vehicle maintenance, and building cleaning and catering. The Department is proud of its high standards of performance and how it has continuously improved that performance whilst having a cost conscious stance for its taxpayers. Waste services, street cleansing services and refuse collection services are all outsourced to commercial contract. An internal body to the Council known as the Operational Services Unit provides similar cleansing services as an internal support to the Council. It has proved so efficient that this unit does work for other County Council departments, such as playground maintenance, graffiti removal, portable appliance testing, litter bin maintenance and signage.

The study has been developed over a two-year period and has watched the City Council not only take advantage of new products available but has tried to include all parties that might be able to inform the debate about environmentally friendly operation of Council services.

Background to the Case

The environment has become a complex issue that is gathering momentum. The pressure to manage environmental issues has increased for all organisations over the past five years or more. Each public sector body has had to determine how they are going to face such environmental issues. New policies have been developed in terms of procuring goods and services for the organisation. All organisations can be perceived to have a high or low environmental risk depending on the amount of the energy levels consumed by the organisation for instance in manufacture or similar conversion process of raw material to finished product. In this instance the City Council is not only responsible for its own organisational behaviour but of all of its inhabitants. Similarly the sustainability of the raw materials used within the organisation may affect the level of risk. A major focus for every individual whether in private sector business, public sector departments or agencies or private citizens is the ability and willingness to reuse or recycle products bought, used and disposed of in daily working of domestic life. The disposability of goods is an important factor nowadays and is taken into account in their design much more so than in previous years.

The purchasing function within county councils in general is becoming increasingly more important in terms of their role in cost savings and reductions of waste for local government. Local councils have been affected by the general government move to outsource many of their services rather than to operate in-house teams of direct labour organisations. Similarly, procurement as a function operating within a wider supply network of suppliers external to the council and those internal working parties in the council, the purchasers have the opportunity to influence and manage the organisation's environmental performance. Procurement contracts for cleaning services can impact significantly upon environmental management performance within the organisation and act as a clear signal to members of the public about the council's performance and how the council might expect them to respond to the demands of the environment in which they live.

When properly handled, environmental procurement promotes awareness across the entire supply chain of the importance attached to the need for less environmentally damaging products to be made available. The purchaser at each stage of the procurement process should consider the effects of the acquisition on the environment and evaluate this as part of the route towards making a final decision.

The local authorities are subject to the same European procurement legislation that central government must use to procure goods and services. This means that all services in respect of waste management that are being placed in the open market for delivery must be competitively tendered. The procurement team of this Council have been working hard over the past five years to develop an innovative approach to obtaining the vast services required in the waste management for the Borough. Unfortunately, the entire competitive exercise was aborted through frustrating delays in obtaining planning permission for new landfill sites for example and because the economics of removing waste and recycling waste products is changing as new technology is developed and other resources become scarcer. There are plans to develop several contracts in the future but the Council have decided, in the meantime, to try to develop a more comprehensive strategy, after a review of all services, for all of the needs as identified in this study. To allow time for the proposals for an integrated and sustainable waste management solution to be drawn up, for and by the Council, a limited extension of the operational life of the existing programme of waste removal and disposal has been arranged. The Council estimate that a further £20million of capital investment is required whilst the new plans are developed to help to make safe the existing landfill site for access and future pollution control. The progress on development of the new integrated strategy has been slow but a meeting in late 2000 has raised the profile of the matter in terms of cost and urgency for resolution.

Factors for Consideration in the Development of the Requirement

Volumes of Household Rubbish

Around 300,000 people and over 150,000 families live within the borough of East Abbeyworth. Each year the Council collects around 150,000 tons of rubbish and waste. The average family in this area throws out 30kg of rubbish into their Council-allocated bin every week. This works out over one ton of rubbish per family per year. The rubbish can be classified into different categories such as garden and food waste, dust, paper and card, plastic, glass, metals and cloth.

In addition to these quantities of rubbish the Council have identified various sites where members of the public can take their own rubbish to recycling centres. These vary from council to council but this Council offers recycling facilities for garden waste, paper, glass, engine oil, tins and cans, cloth, scrap metal and fridges and freezers. Some 32 of these centres exist throughout the Council at amenity sites or in supermarket car parks.

One quarter on the entire waste produced by the population of East Abbeyworth is food and garden refuse. These types of waste are what are known as biodegradable which means that they rot naturally in time. There is an opportunity to utilise this waste as compost that can be reused on the ground. A campaign is commencing later this year to encourage people to develop their own compost with the waste produced from their own households as this would provide a useful by-product and reduce the costs of removal of waste by bin lorries etc.

Litter

Litter is rubbish thrown in the wrong place; it includes sweet papers, cigarette ends and empty packets, chewing gum, plastic bags and glass. Apart from the fact that litter makes the streets look untidy it can also be dangerous to humans and animals.

It costs the Council some £8million a year to have the streets cleaned of thousands of tons of unsightly and unhygienic litter. The Council prefers to encourage and persuade people in preventing litter but use an army of litter wardens to use its powers to prosecute offenders to remove this costly blight on the streets. The Council have made a law against dropping litter and the consequences of doing so, if caught, are a £2500 fine. In 1998 over 50 people were prosecuted for causing litter in the borough.

Another main source of litter is that of dog mess. In the county council area studied there are over 12,000 licensed dogs. Dog mess in children's play areas or on the footpath can be very unpleasant. Complaints have been received at the Council about such mess getting on children's pushchairs, on wheelchairs and on peoples shoes. This type of waste has been known to cause blindness in children. Again a fine has been levied of £500 on those owners who do not clean up their dogs' mess from a public place.

The Streets and Rubbish

There are some 844 kilometres of streets in this Council domain. The Council makes sure that the streets are kept clean and tidy. Street cleaning costs over £6million every year, again paid for by the residents from the

Council rates demand. There are performance targets placed upon the Council by central government that are passed on to the Council's contractors to clean the streets within a set time period of them being made dirty. The busier the area, such as a shopping centre area where members of the public are frequently using the site, the quicker the target clean-up period imposed. This is of course outside of the regular cleansing activity which is undertaken daily. In total there are four different contractual arrangements to ensure the Council's street cleansing obligations are met. These are road sweepers, team sweepers, orderlies with litter pickers and brushes and devices called green machines that wash and sweep the streets at the same time. Graffiti and bill posting cause all manner of problems for the Council and the removal of them is an important aspect of the Council cleaning contractors work.

Environmental Protection

A separate but associated department of the Council known as environmental protection tackles other sorts of waste and nuisance caused or generated by the waste and litter left by members of the public on the thoroughfare. These are aspects of air pollution through bonfires, accumulations of refuse on private land and other forms of statutory nuisance. A body of pest control operators control infestations of rodents, fleas, cockroaches and wasps. Whilst these activities are seemingly outside the control of the HESD, they work closely with this environmental protection unit as there workloads are interrelated.

Natural Resources

The County Council believe that throwing things away is wasteful. Natural resources such as coal and oil are used to make most of the goods that we buy. Much information has been circulating from many research bodies and government institutions about the need to save those natural resources so that there will be some of them in the future.

Disposal of Waste Materials

There are strict legal requirements surrounding the disposal of rubbish particularly where the rubbish is to be tipped on open ground. Every bin full of rubbish has to be emptied into a bin lorry, and taken to one of the authorised landfill sites. A landfill site, a disused quarry, is an area that can be filled in and used for other purposes. The landfill site has been lined with heavy-duty waterproof liners so that the rotting rubbish and dirty water do not leak into local rivers and streams. The rotting rubbish produces a gas called methane that can be collected and utilised for electricity. The dirty water is drained off and treated before release. These landfill sites are chosen for the particular purpose of developing them or reclaiming land. They are not plentiful especially in inner city built up areas away from the sea or shorelines.

Costs

For every ton of waste disposed of in such a landfill tip there is a cost of £70. The money to support the removal of waste comes from the council rates charged to each household. In the year 2001 this Council is trying to reduce the amount of rubbish taken to the Council landfill tip by as much as 15%.

It stands to reason that if we as citizens did not throw away as much rubbish then we could save monies on both the disposal costs and the utilisation of the materials themselves as part of a programme of reuse or recycling. The council provide guidance on things that can be done to reduce waste, reuse things and recycle, such as buying products in larger containers rather than smaller ones, and buying refills and avoiding goods with lots of packaging layers. Similarly, we can reuse items for other things than for their original purpose. Recycling offers the opportunity to clean and break items and make them into something new. This activity saves energy, water and raw materials and reduces pollution,

Health Issues

As identified above, the sheer volumes of waste and litter discarded in the Council area raises significant health issues for the Council. As the profile for the waste management is high, so too is the management of health concerns aroused from the disposal of waste in the area.

Stakeholders

There are many stakeholders involved in the process of waste removal and disposal. Central government imposes performance levels upon local councils, who impose performance levels on contractors. Each taxpayer and visitor to the borough has a vested interest in the service provision. Cleaning material manufacturers along with cleansing machinery suppliers etc all have a role to play. Silent stakeholders are the many animals and birds that use the area in a different way to the members of the public but nevertheless have the right to clean and conservation approaches taken to the country life.

Customer Complaints Procedure

Customers of the Council are mainly the residents and business owners of property in the area. There are also visitors to the Borough who have to be given a safe, friendly, clean and pollution- free environment in which to go about their business. Most of the customers pay an annual rates bill to cover the work of the Council. They have the right to expect clean, safe environments. In line with the customer focus of the Council a complaints procedure has been drawn up to deal with issues where members of the public are dissatisfied with the service given. Council policy is to view complaints about any of its services as an opportunity to learn from its customers and thus improve the quality of service that it delivers. The information about the number and nature of complaints and indeed how these are dealt with are freely published in the Council's annual report for all to read.

Similarly, customers are extremely reluctant to enter into recycling and reusing plans that the Council needs to lay down in order to maintain reasonable rates and manage the environmental pressures placed upon them. Given the amount of waste and litter production by people in the Council area, it is a significant task to persuade the public to curb their habits to 'throw out' all items. There are of course amongst the population those environmentally friendly individuals who do take their recycling waste to the designated centres; however, these are lesser than the rest of the throw-away members of the population. Such recycling costs are therefore higher as there is less profit in the lower amounts collected whilst the system of collecting such waste from the general bin system is still high.

The Council waste management programme and the vast team of workers who are engaged in the process are almost invisible. In modern society the waste is created and almost as if by magic it disappears each week. Publicity about waste management and the environment is slow to break into the consciousness of people. If the system of clearance operates smoothly people almost take it for granted.

However when the system breaks down or cannot cope with the excess amounts, for instance at Christmas, then the people notice and mount complaints. Most people would be surprised if at all interested in finding out the volumes of waste produced by each household each year. The people's role in the generation of it seems in some cases to go unnoticed.

Role of the Procurement in the Organisation

The Council has adopted an environmental procurement policy. The contribution therefore that the function makes as alluded to earlier is important. Firstly, the issue of assessing suppliers and contractors to the Council in this arena is important from an aspect of examining potential environmental consequences of using a particular supplier. The materials chosen for purposes of cleansing or disposing of waste or its by-products is a feature of the procurement that must be considered early. When buying products the procurement function on behalf of the Council must concern itself about the lifetime costs of owning and running the product, particularly cleansing machinery for example. In line with the Council's commitment to 'best value' the decision to buy must revolve around the factors of cost not price. Therefore the justification to purchase a higher-priced item can be made in terms of energy consumption rates, and consequent increases in wastage and disposal factors. A clear criterion in the design of products and the choice of off-the-shelf products should be the ability to recycle it or dispose of it safely. Particularly important in the design of such services as are highlighted in this study, is the consumption levels of non-renewable resources associated with the service, ie landfill sites or methane gas production from the waste decomposition. The inefficient use of fuel or energy has to be considered in terms of both environmental and other constraints upon the Council and the market in meeting the service requirement.

Part of the policy identified by the Council in its guidance on recycling and reusable containers etc for the public is carried through in its own procurement plans. Throwaway dispensers and aerosols are not the preference of the Council. This means that the price charged to the Council may be more but the costs work out considerably less in the long run in many ways. Another key issue for designing the nature and practice of services in waste management is the extent and nature of the emissions from the equipment or products under normal use and under situations of abuse.

An important distinction between recycled and environmentally friendly products used in environmentally consciously designed services is a major concern for procurement professionals in the Council arena of waste management. The entire Council activity promotes and develops environmental issues in its working practice and in its dealings with suppliers.

Conclusions

This case is put forward as an example of a complex service area with many emotive aspects in the management and disposal of waste and waste products for the Council domain of East Abbeyworth. Whilst the procurement itself has not been discussed or mapped formally, many aspects of worth to designers and purchasers have been identified for consideration. The Council decided during the competitive tendering process to abort the current attempts to finalise contract plans in favour of stepping back to examine a new strategic review of waste management in the Council. The plan was to move toward the development of an integrated and sustainable waste management policy for the Council that would permit an effective and cost-conscious service; consideration of the environmental issues as well as more modern methods of waste management could therefore be taken into account. Issues of environmental policy, constraints of the market and on the Council placed by individual ratepayer's expectation frame the way the services can operate. The processes involved in the removal of waste from homes, recycling centres, streets, roads, etc are complex and costly. Think about the way the waste removal service operates in your area. Think about the amount of rubbish that you and your household generate. Work out the process for removal of waste alone and then multiple this by the amount of litter to be collected etc.

The purpose of the case is to introduce a complex services area that demands many different elements to be considered in the development of the contracts of procurement. Both goods and services are required aplenty to meet the needs of the Abbeyworth Council and its population. Consider the study area and try to determine the many different design factors that need to be taken into account, some of which are not mentioned here, in the development of the services to manage waste. Consider the number of stakeholders involved in the process.

Case Synopsis

This case study identifies issues for consideration in the design of future contracts for the procurement of cleaning services for the purpose of waste management on local authority streets and domestic homes in the Council area of East Abbeyworth in England. The case is put forward as a design and 'environmentally friendly' approach to the procurement of cleaning services. Students are invited to identify the design issues and comment upon how they might be addressed and on how they could impact the development of the service design to ensure that the council concerned meets all of the responsibilities. The approach to this matter follows an initiative across all county councils to ensure that the development of such contracts remains within government guidelines for the environmental procurement of materials and services pertinent to the cleaning services task. Waste management issues occupy a prominent place in the council business.

Teaching and Learning Objectives

- To provide students with the opportunity to understand a complex case requiring best practice in the public sector procurement arena that explicitly incorporates design concepts early in its procurement strategy.
- To provide students with the basis for a discussion on the procurement path taken and the importance of design to both the product, service and the supply chain behind it all.

- To help students understand areas of synergy between design criteria for the development of new products and the procurement criteria for the development of sound procurement decisions.

- To explore the importance of involving key stakeholders in the procurement process throughout.

Main Issues Raised

- Consideration of design concepts
- Consideration of the impact of design upon the identification of need
- Consideration of design upon the finished procurement contract
- Consideration of procurement decision criteria
- Consideration of the importance of external and internal interface in the development of the requirement for procurement.

Specific Questions

1. Consider how design factors will feature in the planning of strategic procurement planning.

2. Pugh's Model of Design Boundaries provided in the introduction to this book, cited 'design' and 'procurement' criteria that should be considered in the development of new product. Consider how important the inclusion of these criteria is to the success of this entire service development project.

3. Identify the involvement of the various stakeholders in this case study process and explain the role that they played in the development of final framework.

4. Draw a flow diagram to show the stages of involvement of these stakeholders through the development of the framework process.

The Approach Taken

The case was approached from the perspective of design issues and how they have been integrated into the procurement strategy of this contract within the East Abbeyworth County Council. The full approach in terms of questioning and method for the development of the case study has been incorporated into the chapter of introduction in this text. The Pugh Model of Design Boundaries has been used to identify the main elements considered in new product design and those most pertinent to criteria for making decisions for various procurements throughout both the private and public sectors. This model was described at the outset of the interview for the collection of data for this case study. It was also discussed throughout the case study research to help identify the extent to which the design and procurement factors mesh together in the development of a new product where the innovation of suppliers is required to ensure that the end product is suitable for the purpose designated for it.

The contractual approach taken to the services for waste management could not be mapped as the approach to the procurement was ceased in favour of a more strategic review and integrated plan being devised. Nevertheless, the study throws up some interesting design areas for consideration when developing a complex service contractual approach such as this.

Companion Lecturer's Aid for Public Sector Design Case Studies

Introduction

This chapter has been designed to provide a companion study aid tool to be used in conjunction with the case studies in this book.

There are many areas where the public sector procurement function can benefit from using design thinking and design processes within the context of their role in procurement of goods and services and in the management of the supply chain. Design impacts upon three fundamental issues: function, economics and aesthetics. Improved design effectiveness within the public sector could force down costs; ensure compliance with both legislation and standards; impact positively upon 'green procurement' and improve quality of life. To achieve design effectiveness there needs to be a recognition by buyers that more emphasis needs to be placed on the initial clarification of the user's requirements and the better capture and integration of those requirements. This would produce a more cohesive structured specification format compatible with the functionality of the design process that would then align product availability and user requirements. Design can therefore be used to better effect on both buyer's and seller's sides of the market place.

In the context of this book we are concerned with the 'design' of products and services for utilisation within public sector business activity. In general terms we tend to think of a product as a tangible physical object like a piece of furniture or a storage cabinet perhaps. A service implies a more intangible experience such as security, cleaning or a training event. However, most if not all things that we buy are comprised of a combination of products and services. There may be 'delivery', 'after sales service' or 'maintenance' required with furniture procurement and there are various products required for use during the delivery of the security service such as uniforms, keys, torches communication radios, etc.

A product or service is anything that can be offered to customers in order to satisfy their needs and expectations. There are three levels relating to such satisfaction: those of expected benefits that the customer is buying; the component products and services that are bought and; the processes gone through to achieve delivery. The process is vitally important, as it is the operation that creates the products and services puts them together into packages and delivers them to the customer to fulfil the need.

Thus the design of a product or service and the development of the concept for procurement of goods and services have much to link them. Each of the case studies discussed in this book begins with the generation of a concept and the development of a requirement that is considered throughout the procurement of that product or service. As the cases are based in the public sector there are no internal manufacturing or service provision facilities; all procurement contracts deal with the development of the requirement and the buying of that requirement into the sector to provide for the needs already identified. From this perspective the procurement function is much more likely to be involved in the generation of the initial concept than if the organisation discussed, actually manufactured or delivered the services themselves. The public sector in the main has neither design function nor manufacturing function and all of the cases are examining the development of contracts for provision to members of the public.

Nowadays, the market conveys that the look and feel of products and services is important. The finished product or service is seen as potentially the most effective point of sale marketing tool ever devised. It is very important, then, that the product or service meets the 'right need' given the importance placed upon it as a main vehicle to gain or maintain competitive position in the market. These issues may not be deemed as pertinent within the public sector arena. However, rather than gaining competitive advantage there would be significant benefits for Value For Money from meeting the 'right need'; similarly customer satisfaction is much more prevalent as government departments, agencies and local authorities serve the needs of taxpayers, so design is therefore a vital criterion. Public sector procurement staffs are buying from the wider market and so the method of thinking used by designers must impact upon the development of the requirement initially as well as ultimately upon the choice of procurement of goods and services.

Thus, familiarity with the thinking involved in the designing process is important not only for those engaged in designing, but for anyone desirous of developing the requirement for the 'right' product or service. This in fact could include anyone involved in managing the supply chain and/or marshalling the market's production of goods and services for their organisation's internal use.

Leading design practitioners concern themselves with the entire customer-product relationship and its lifecycle. The product experience for a customer begins before the first stage of awareness of the product when in fact neither a positive or negative opinion exists. Familiarity with the product brings a reaction, possibly a purchase and eventually disposal.

Product designers are now also guided by the thinking that a product's functionality establishes a company's reputation. This aspect is equally important for the public sector business image especially where members of the public are involved with the service provided. The increasing importance attached by companies to customer relations explains this shift in thinking. Proper management of the product design is therefore vital.

In all of the cases studied there was a need to involve many different stakeholders in the process of designing the requirement; to include users and those with vested interest in the design impacted greatly upon the overall procurement. Integration of procurement design and individuals in the process has proven to improve the procurement outcome.

Aim of the Book

The aim of the book is to offer lecturers and their students examples of current 'best practice' procurement processes that have included design factors in the development of contracts or offer considerable opportunity to those lecturers and students to suggest a design for a service that is rich in design issues, within the public sector. Two key tenets upon which the book is based are:

- The consideration of design issues early in the procurement cycle.
- The involvement of many individuals throughout the development of the requirement so as to provide a wide view of the impact of the goods or services to be procured upon the users and to ensure a closer assessment of the 'right' goods or service for the procurement.

It is the intention of the book to lead by good example of the ways in which design should be considered at the early stages of procurement from the concept development or the development of specification phase, and how this development trawls widely upon various individuals and organisations connected in some way with the procured item, which leads to sound and appropriate purchases of goods or services.

Purchasers implicitly consider many of the design factors pertinent in the development of contracts during the evaluation of products offered from the market place. However, when they are made more explicit early in the consideration of product or service requirement there is an improvement in the end product or service choice. The cases cited in the book explain the way the procurement has been handled but emphasise the design issues and how they have been or need to be incorporated into the procurement contracts let for the case scenarios. Students should be invited to identify and extrapolate design issues from procurement criteria within the study and to consider the impact that these have made upon the overall development of the procurement outcome. Specific questions are asked. If this design issue was not considered how would the contract have looked? How important were the various design issues to the procurement? What might have been the outcome had the specific design issues not been considered in the development of the procurement plan?

Generally speaking, knowledge of what influences product design, customer choice, the design processes and management issues pertinent to the acquisition of goods and services will serve to make more rounded procurement professionals who will ultimately be better equipped to perform many tasks required of them in today's buying world.

Audiences and Uses of the Cases

The cases are suitable for final year undergraduate and post-graduate students on a variety of courses including:

- Supply chain management
- Strategic purchasing
- Organisational behaviour
- General management, eg MBA.

Students need to be aware of the concepts of strategy, design concepts and public sector procedures before attempting the cases.

It is suggested that the lecturer divide the course into groups of around five to six at most and they should then be asked to give a presentation on how they see the case scenario and how they would deal with specific questions and issues raised with each case.

The Case Studies

The organisations that have cooperated in the development of the case studies are:

- Inland Revenue, England
- Driver and Vehicle Licensing Agency, S. Wales
- Belfast City Council, Northern Ireland
- Driving Test Standards Agency, England
- Government Purchasing Agency, Northern Ireland
- Waste Management in a local council.

Case Study Structure

The case studies have been developed using a structured approach:

- Defining the aims of the public sector department or agency discussed
- Defining the aims and purpose of specific procurement ie what was to be achieved in buying the specific procurement
- Examining how the specification or requirement documents were put together and the factors of design and procurement that were considered in its development.
- Examining the process and interactions of relevant 'stakeholders' in the procurement process, ie purchasing, users, industry, engineers, designers, finance etc
- Explaining the outcome and level of success from the procurement, ie benefits and objectives achieved or issues that could be improved
- Identifying lessons learnt, ie why the procurement process was good or bad in its approach.

Case Study Approach

A set of clear objectives has been set for the investigation of the cases:

- A clear set of design parameters and boundaries
- A clear role for procurement within the organisation
- To cite the implications for incorrect purchases and the importance of the procurement to the organisation as a whole
- To focus on the technical/user interface in the identification and management of need established for the specific procurement
- To develop a perspective of the interface between the various stakeholders using the following stances:

    Product/requirement definition

    Process operation and management

    Technical detail and complexity

    People factors

    Communication

    Organisation.

Theories for Design and Procurement

The book draws heavily upon an early design model generated by Pugh in 1991, that highlights the main boundaries around which designing a new product should revolve. This has been expanded to consider these criteria in service design. In the course of research, the author has conducted interviews and questionnaires using this model to discuss the issue of design and its importance amongst the purchasing fraternity. It was clear from the surveys that many purchasers felt that design was only relevant in the procurement of print or construction, or to products that required a very technical response and to a lesser degree furniture but mostly from an ergonomic point of view. Some terms, for instance, functionality, total acquisition cost, maintainability were quoted as important to purchasers; these terms would be familiar to procurement staff in the criteria that they use everyday. Some of the more specific design terminology, for instance aesthetics, re-styling, ornamentation shape etc did not score highly as important to them. The term 'design' has not been seen to be rolling off the tongue easily of many purchasers in the public sector, except to mean aesthetics or appearance.

However, many of the terms used in Pugh's model are known to purchasers as procurement criteria pertinent to the development of a specification and certainly taken into account in the evaluation of the competitive bids made from potential suppliers in tendering exercises. This is clear too in the cited case studies within the main text associated with this companion book. These criteria need to be seen as design issues and evaluated much earlier in the development of the requirement. These exemplary cases show just how these factors have been included from the perspective of design recognition as well as considered in the overall procurement criterion during the development of the contract. If this is effected then the procured goods or services contract may well be made more accessible to a wider population. For instance, the inclusion of a wider number of goods categories within the government procurement card or the detailed thought on the various sensitivities at the crematorium blended with the need to ensure a timely and efficient service and the design of the touch-screen theory test that included not only the IT phobic but the many cultural languages within the country.

Pugh (1991) believes that all design should start from the identification of user need and that when this is satisfied the product will fit into the required environment. Underpinning this belief is the need to develop a 'product brief' or product specification. Many 'stakeholders' and factors are involved in the development of this specification. Pugh's Design Boundaries Model (Fig 1) shows 32 different facets of the business environment that can be taken into account during the development of the specification document. This model is used in this research to represent the basis of design thinking required to develop a product or service specification.

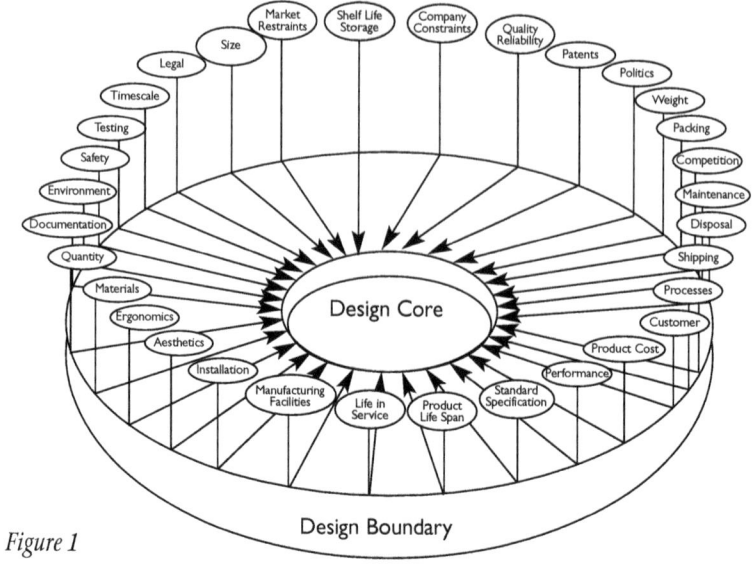

Figure 1

Each of these criterion appears to greater or lesser extent in the case studies. Each has an importance as expressed by the procurement professionals in the design of the procurement. Some of these criteria are explicit and others are implicit in the design of the service or goods discussed. Students should seek these out and discuss them in the context of the overall procurement as highlighted previously. F

Turning to the procurement focus within which design thinking is to be seated, the theorist Saunders (1997) in his text used within the CIPS Graduate Diploma qualification on the subject of Strategic Purchasing offers a 'Supply Chain Strategy Framework'. The purpose of this framework is to position the various business strategies that need to be coordinated to greater or lesser degree within the management of the supply chain as they relate to the wider corporate mission statement and goals for the organisation. Saunders's framework has been reproduced below. Public sector purchasers are taught how businesses operate along the supply chain.

As can be seen from the diagram of the framework Saunders identifies design strategy as a separate entity informing the product development activity. There is no link displayed either between the design and supply chain strategy nor from their source disciplines of design and procurement. The only feed of knowledge of both these strategies is drawn through the product strategy. It would therefore very much depend on whether the business operating such a strategy framework adopted an integrated approach to the development of a product as to how much communication would be made between disciplines at product development strategy level. Similarly, the involvement of many individuals in the design of the product will be affected by the way design and the supply functions amongst others work together; this according to the design process theory ultimately affects the outcome of the design and thus the procurement. The public sector, as already alluded to, does not operate with this discipline or functional approach internal to the organisation, nevertheless the awareness of design in the development of the specification internally within in the organisation and how the product or service is designed and requirements are understood by the design fraternity external to the organisation is important

Nevertheless, the role that the procurement function has in the product design process is not easily visible within this model. Also the great bearing that design can have upon the identification of need and the development of a product specification at the early phases of the design process, and the eventual procurement of materials, components or whole goods for the business can not be effective through such a framework as there is no direct contact between the design and procurement functions within it. It has been shown already that there are benefits to be gained through such contact. Indeed that is one of the main reasons why the MOD reviewed their procurement process, to achieve gains witnessed in the USA where it had already been identified that there was the need for procurement and design to work more in line with each other. This framework would not suggest an integrated approach to the management of the product design process that also suggests limited contact between defined disciplines. Whilst Saunders did not include this framework in his text with the intention of drawing any specific link between disciplines, it does nevertheless expose the relationship or lack of one between these functions.

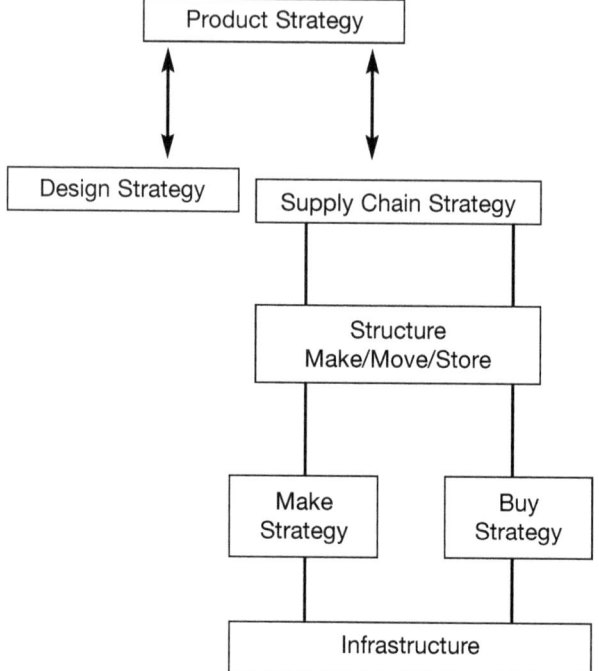

Figure 2

Another model of the strategic supply chain framework, shown in figure 2 above, has been drawn from the perspective of the procurement function to try to better incorporate the role that each of the disciplines has within their respective functions and to demonstrate how they should relate and gain knowledge from each other in a more integrated manner.

One way of improving the design effectiveness in the procurement of goods and services in the public sector would be to ensure the earliest incorporation of design principles within the procurement process and management of the supply chain. It is essential to view design, design processes and design management in a broader context and to re-examine where the impact of design can be felt within business and particularly within the procurement of goods and services.

An examination of the idea generation and product concept within the design processes has shown many interesting approaches to, for instance, the identification of need and product specification that could provide further help to the procurement function to add value to these phases within the 'procurement cycle'.

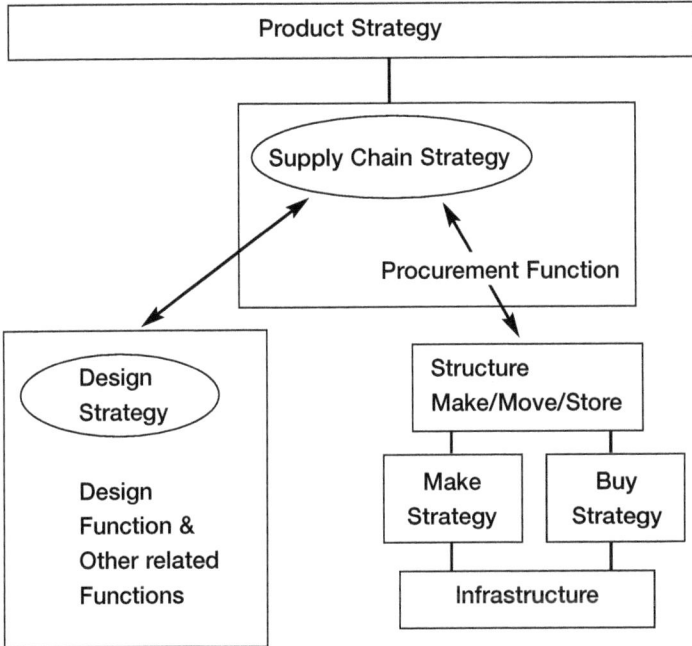

Figure 3

Hughes, Cox and Ralf (1997), developed the model reproduced in figure 3 to demonstrate the need for closer integration of purchasing initiatives with business-led supplier management in specific business case studies that necessitated a radical shift in the role of the procurement function within those organisations. However, for the purposes of this book I feel it does demonstrate an integrated approach as this model offers a modern view of process or activity relationships within the organisation, albeit coordinated in effort for a specific goal of supplier management.

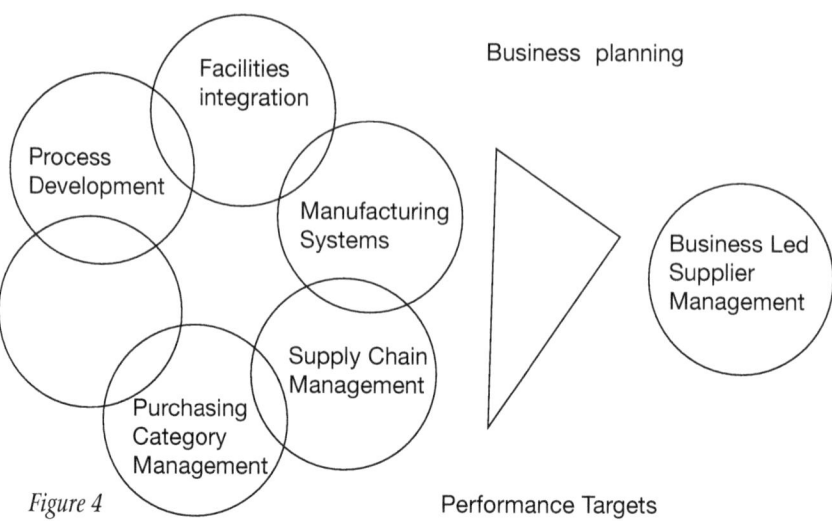

Figure 4

Whilst the various functions involved in these activities are not explicitly mentioned and the categories of activity do not all overlap each other, there is a coordinated direction through business planning and performance targets. Therefore there is an implied multi-functional approach at least in respect of output and goals.

It is clear then that there needs to be a closer link between procurement and design thinking and that an integrated approach across business is required to effect this. The criteria displayed in Pugh's model can show fundamental design concerns for purchasers in the public sector. As seen from the case studies in the associated book these design/procurement criteria are considered in exemplar fashion in the government procurement of goods and services cited. The involvement of the many and varied stakeholders in the procurement process during the development of the requirement was seen as important, too.

Case Study – Inland Revenue Furniture Procurement

Case Synopsis

This true case describes the generation of a 'new look' furniture framework contract currently used within the Inland Revenue (IR) and the Customs and Excise Department of the UK central government. The departments seized the opportunity to fully consider the furniture requirements in light of organisational changes and more modern working patterns operating in the public and private sectors, such as team meetings and home working. In this furniture framework IR sought wider opportunities for Value For Money. They also saw this as an opportunity to enhance the staff working environment and morale in IR overall by showing the staff their value in considering new forms of office environments and working arrangements. IR too wished to be seen as a good employer who provides practical working environments and one that listens to its staff on what is needed to perform the many tasks asked off it. The plan was to also offer the staff the right to choose their own furniture and to design their working space that they hoped would add value to IR as a whole. The approach that was taken to the development of the contract to back up their furniture requirements was innovative and IR sought to learn from past 'mistakes' by seeking to embark on a strategic procurement path and to explicitly include design concepts and criteria in the framework and specification design. They also wished to exploit external and internal expertise and experience in the development of this framework document. This approach shows a model strategic procurement approach:

- Planning ahead
- Incorporating a broad understanding of organisation, market and

product criteria in the development of the framework document
- Learning from the past
- Considering stakeholders' views
- Working with suppliers and industry
- Adding value to the process by working on cost not just price.

In addition the strengths of the work and the success factors for this project have been attributed to the broad consideration of design issues early on in the development process and by reviewing the work done to ensure effective best practice in procurement in the future.

The Approach Taken

The case has been written with full cooperation of Inland Revenue's Central Procurement Team. The case was approached from the perspective of design issues and how they had or had not been incorporated into the procurement strategy of IR. The full approach in terms of questioning and method has been incorporated into the chapter of introduction in this text. The Pugh Model of Design Boundaries has been used to identify the main elements considered in new product design and those most pertinent to criteria for making decisions for various procurements throughout both the private and public sectors. This model was identified at the end of the interview with a representative of IR's Central Procurement Team.

Teaching and Learning Objectives

- To provide students with the opportunity to understand a case relaying best practice in the public sector procurement arena that explicitly incorporates design concepts early in its procurement strategy.

- To help students understand areas of synergy between design criteria for the development of new products and the procurement criteria for the development of sound procurement decisions.
- To provide scope to analyse the design issues considered in the development of a furniture framework.
- To examine the effect of design on procurement strategies.
- To explore the importance of involving key stakeholders in the procurement process throughout.

Main Issues Raised

There were many issues raised by this case study but the important aspects lay in the consideration of:

- the impact of design upon the identification of need and upon the finished procurement contract
- procurement decision criteria
- the value of procurement research
- key elements of strategic procurement
- the importance of external and internal interface in the development of the requirement for procurement
- the impact of organisational values, mission and culture upon procurement/design decisions
- EC procurement Directives
- issues such as Intellectual Property Rights and legal factors in the development of procurement contracts.

Specific Questions

1. Consider the IR case study in the light of the Pugh Model of Design Boundaries provided in the introduction to this companion book, to determine how many and in what depth the cited 'design' and 'procurement' criteria were considered in the development of this furniture framework.

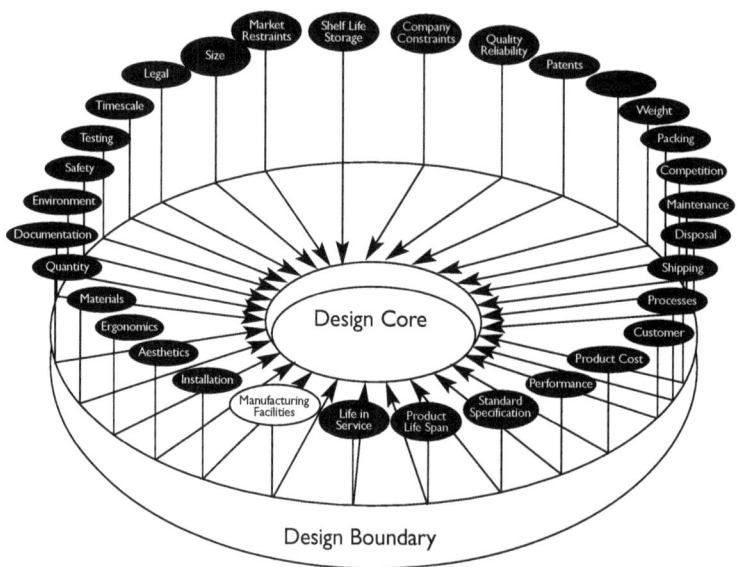

Notes:

As can be seen from this adaptation of Pugh's model many of the design issues established are included in the case study. Students should be encouraged to trace these to specific data described in the case. This case is design-rich and many of the issues with some 29 criteria being included.

The weighting given to these criteria is subjective and cannot be prioritised, however students should identify the following aspects in relation to the identification of the criteria in the case:

- The entire purpose of the design of the procurement requirement was to meet a need established in the department of Inland Revenue to enhance the ever-reducing in size internal environment and to work within the market restraints to meet that need.
- Cost was obviously a key factor expressed in the reduction of waste and improved quality/ reliability of the furniture itself to provide a higher level of performance.
- The specification was not standard as many offices were used for different purposes and staff worked differently.
- Aesthetics and ergonomics were key and a new office layout was adopted with the new furniture designs chosen for the contract.
- Materials chosen for the furniture had to be lighter (less weighty), and smaller than previous furniture used in IR and had to be durable with a recommended life in service
- Legal issues were pertinent to the competitive process under which the furniture contract was let and in respect of the intellectual property (patents) owned by each supplier in the furniture designs.
- Politics featured in the development of the contract and related to the people, culture and permitted use and design of furniture for IR.
- Time was only a factor in so far as IR took time to develop the right approach and design approach rather than rushing to develop the contract through pressure from either users or management.
- Testing was an innovative approach used in the government contract used to include staff (customer) and development an ownership of the new designs and to ensure the 'road worthiness' of each design and office layout for the customer. IR took a very customer-focused approach to the whole procurement.
- Documentation competition and processes are always important in government buying as the audit trail has to be transparent through the expenditure of taxpayers' monies.
- Storage was an issue in this procurement as the items were bulky and needed to be more easily transported and stored than previous designs.

- Quantity was an issue in the levels of procurement of the items as the numbers of desks etc was reducing as offices in many towns were closing and new style offices changed the needs for working practices to be as before.
- Disposal issues on all procurement items must be assessed.

2. Consider how important the inclusions of these criteria are to the success of the entire project.

Students should be able to derive the importance of each factor from the lessons learnt in the cases by the procurement team. Each had an importance but some examples follow.

- The inclusion of the users in the development of the furniture contract helped the environmental issues certainly come to the fore but eventually aided the acceptance of the new IR culture and the new furniture designs.
- The inclusion of procurement research into the design and the availability of furniture ensured that they knew what the market restraints were to supplying the products they sought and helped them to consider issues such as aesthetics, ergonomics, weight, maintenance, disposal, size, installation etc.
- The power of the customer in procurement and design decisions especially today with the customer-driven supply chain is important.

3. Identify the involvement of the various stakeholders in this case study process and explain the role that they played in the development of final framework.

- Central Procurement Team IR: they were central to the entire generation of the contract approach:

- Departmental Procurement Team – Customs and Excise: they played a lesser role in the development of the design of the approach and the choices made, however were instrumental by joining with IR in obtaining the discounts that made the various choices of furniture possible for the government contract.
- Estate Unit Customs and Excise: played a lesser role in defining the Customs and Excise requirements for the central procurement team to include them in the requirement specification and quantities.
- Space Planning Unit IR: this unit was fundamental in collating the requirements across the department and in offering a service for the design of the office layout. The space planning unit also ran the testing facility and trial of the furniture at its offices in Nottingham. The survey data was collected by this unit during the survey.
- Industry – FIRA and Trade Associations – OFMA: these organisations were crucial to the development of the requirement and to the determination of the market restraints in the design of the contract.
- Furniture suppliers: the furniture suppliers were involved mostly once the requirement had been developed although a secret recognisance was undertaken by IR procurement staff to examine furntiure at an early stage. At the competitive tendering stage of the process, suppliers were invited to supply 'sample office layouts' for internal IR staff to consider. It was interesting to note that the image of the supplier was one of 'hard sell' and this affected the utilisation of the additonal services gained on the contract for office planning.
- Regional Office Staff: these staff were deemed crucial in the process of design and procurement if the contract was to be a success. There were many political and cultural issues at work in the department and the furniture allocation was seen as a signal of the changes in the environment. Whilst the staff were included at the design and choice of options stage certain staff were not included later due to perceived negative influence that they might have had on the outcome of the

entirely new approach.

- Valuation Agency: this office played a small part in some regards as they merely procured some of IR's old furniture which allowed the new environment to be enhanced at IR. The Valuation Agency's furniture was in worse condition than IR's before the new contract and so this acquired newer furniture for them. This role was one of desirable disposal of furniture within the governemnt system rather than scrap that would have achieved less monies.

- Customers: the concept of the customer is a focal one in this case study. The customer can be many of the parties identified above, such as the regional office staff, the Customs and Excise or IR themselves. At different levels thay will play a different part in the sequence of events that transpired in the development of the contract at IR.

Case Study – Developing a Café at the Belfast City Council

Case Synopsis

This case study was developed with the cooperation of the Belfast City Council. This case explores the practical development of a new waiting area with catering facilities at the crematorium in Northern Ireland. It on first appearance seems to be a straightforward extension of the existing building and a new service provided by the Council. However, it actually proved fraught with complications that had to be managed in a particular way to ensure that the environmental issues, emotions and rites of individuals were preserved. Some interesting aspects were highlighted such as attempting to manage the unpredictable behaviours of people in mourning experienced by crematorium staff. The balance between practicalities and sensitivities in the development of the requirement tested the procurement and consultants.

The case sets the scene of the contract in the aims and role of the Belfast City Council and maps the developments of the contract through public sector competitive tendering regulations. The main benefit of examining this contract was to reveal the considerable design factors that exposed themselves as more research was undertaken and more stakeholders became involved. Seemingly unlikely factors had to be considered in the development of the requirements. There was an advanced approach taken to the award of the contract that differed from the norm in contracts of this nature. Whilst these are not fully explored in the case, it is clear that through the central management approach adopted for the contract benefits in co-ordination and cost reduction were achieved.

The Approach Taken

The case was approached from the perspective of design issues and how they have been integrated into the procurement strategy of this contract within the Belfast City Council. The full approach in terms of questioning and method for the development of the case study has been incorporated into the chapter of introduction in this text. The Pugh Model of Design Boundaries has been used to identify the main elements considered in new product design and those most pertinent to criteria for making decisions for various procurements throughout both the private and public sectors. This model was described at the outset of the interview for the collection of data for this case study. It was also discussed throughout the case study research to help identify the extent to which the design and procurement factors mesh together in the development of a new product where the innovation of suppliers is required to ensure that the end product is suitable for the purpose designated for it.

Teaching and Learning Objectives

- To provide students with the opportunity to explore a case rich in design issues of a wide variety from cultural to financial and logistical matters.
- To provide students a discussion platform in respect of the design criteria for the service and the supply chain behind it all.
- To help students understand areas of synergy between design criteria for the development of new products and the procurement criteria for the development of sound procurement decisions.
- To explore the importance of involving key stakeholders in the procurement process throughout.

Main Issues Raised

- The impact of design upon the identification of need.
- The design effect upon the finished procurement contract.
- The contrast between the sensitivities in the design with the logistical necessities of providing an efficient and effective service.
- The importance of taking into account the user groups views as well as the internal client in the development of the requirement for procurement.

Specific Questions

1. Consider what design factors have featured in the planning of strategic procurement planning.

This case is based in an unusual business environment that throws up many difficult issues that have to be managed so as to maintain a smooth running cremation service. Normally there would be a design plan for a scenario of this nature but the procurement strategy laid out by the procurement director at the City Council explicitly included the design factors that emerged from the commissioned consultation with user groups for the crematorium. The most pertinent design features as put forward by Pugh's model lie in the shaded areas on the model attached.

The experience for the mourners at the crematorium was of prime concern for the procurement team at the City Council. This meant that the primary focus of the procurement was the customer. To this end the consultation prior to the development of the building work itself in the architectural design was very informative. The sensitivities of the purpose of the visit to the crematorium meant that issues such as the aesthetics and the environmental circumstances became integral to the design and procurement. Issues such as colour, sound, layout, smell, etc were important in the setting of the café. Timescale for the development work was important as disruption to the existing services had to be avoided. The timing of usage of the facility too was important as mourners could not be allowed to linger in the café for fear of creating delay to the smooth running operation of the crematorium.

The company constraints were flagged as an important design issue as the prime purpose was the continuous process of the services for cremation. The conflict of interest in the continuous flow and logistical concerns in the business for the funeral directors, florists, and cremation managers weighed against the calm, slow, reflective and serene experience desired by the mourners had to be designed into the facility development. The business of the crematorium had to be maintained, however, the need for such a café service had been identified.

The market restraints in developing such a facility were deemed to be important as the boundaries surrounding the expectation of how, what, where and for whom the café operated were largely dictated by the market and its customers. The Belfast City Council were representatives of that customer base and market place and so had to think of these factors in the procurement of the service to develop the facility.

2. **Discuss the contrast in sensitivity in the design of the café because it was to be based in the crematorium with the logistical issues of providing a vital service.**

Despite the crematorium being surrounded by sensitivities for individuals who have recently experienced bereavement its main purpose is the practical business of cremation of the dead. To operate such a service to members of the public and their family and friends, especially with the trend increasing in numbers, requires discipline in terms of timing, standard of performance, environmental conditions, legality, safety etc. When the survey was completed the main 'workers' at the crematorium depended on a fast turn around to ensure that the process was constant for all mourners and in the delivery of all services. However, the mourners were using the facility in very different circumstances and required time to reflect, reverence and a stately approach to be taken to the delivery of the service. Their state of emotion was more unstable than that of the workforce who provided this service and experienced the ceremony and distress of death on a more regular basis. There needed to be a balance of course but there was a stark contrast between those working in the crematorium environment and those visiting the crematorium to cremate a loved one.

The design issues are important in the delivery of the service from both parties' points of view. Students might spend some time thinking about how these vastly different purposes were managed in the delivery of the cremation service.

3. **Identify the involvement of the various stakeholders in this case study process and explain the role that they played in the development of final framework.**

There were many stakeholders involved in the process:

- The project management team: who were responsible for managing the development of the project throughout from the early involvement of the procurement team and the consultation process to the building of the facility.
- The procurement team: who provided a conduit between the project team manager and the outside world that included suppliers, users and members of the wider community.
- The crematorium staff: who worked in the environment every day and provided the vital experience upon which to base the design of the requirement.
- Mourners: who were deemed to be the customer for the service at the crematorium. Their views and requirements were very important to the design of the facility.
- The funeral directors and florists etc: who relied on the swift nature of their entry and exit from the facility to ensure a continuous service to all of their clients. They too were in a position to inform the debate on the way the café service might affect them and the ultimate

performance of the crematorium.

- The City Council: the City Council and its councilors represented the wider population in the country and therefore had to inform the design and take responsibility for the procurement and the building once complete.

Case Study – Government Procurement Card

Case Synopsis

This case study was developed in cooperation with the Government Procurement Agency in Belfast, Northern Ireland and the procurement team in the Department of Trade and Industry in London, England. The study tracks the important design and procurement factors involved in the design and development of the contract for government procurement charge cards. The case explores how the contract was developed and what factors were important in the design of the service. Important factors such as environment, culture, cost, installation, control and measurement all play a part in the design of the procurement card system. Aesthetics too were important to provide a corporate identity and a distinctive appearance to the card for use by members of DTI staff. The DTI were the front-runners in use of the card and have developed some innovative approaches within the context of government to expand the use of the contract both for their staff and suppliers of product and services to the department. Customer and supplier focus for the design was vital, as the system needed both of them to ensure that the system was available and was utilised. Costs and savings were a major feature in the development of the entire approach as both suppliers and buyers benefited from the system in this regard.

The Approach Taken

The case has been written with full cooperation of the Central Procurement Team of the DTI and the Government Purchasing Agency. The case was approached from the perspective of design issues and how they had or had not been incorporated into the procurement strategy of the government procurement system. The full approach in terms of questioning and method has been incorporated into the chapter of introduction in this text. The Pugh Model of Design Boundaries has been used to identify the main elements considered in new product design and those most pertinent to criteria for making decisions for various procurements throughout both the private and public sectors. This model was identified at the end of the interview with a representative of the DTI's Central Procurement Team.

Teaching and Learning Objectives

- To provide students with the opportunity to study a case study pertinent to the design and development of an innovative new service.
- To help students understand areas of synergy between design criteria for the development of new services and the procurement criteria for the development of sound procurement decisions.
- To examine the effect of design on procurement strategies.
- To explore the importance of involving key stakeholders in the procurement process throughout.

Main Issues Raised

- Consideration of design concepts
- Consideration of design upon the finished procurement contract
- Consideration of the value of procurement research
- Consideration of key elements of strategic procurement
- Consideration of the importance of external and internal interface in the development of the requirement for procurement
- Consideration of supplier/buyer relationships.

Specific Questions

1. Consider the GPC case study in the light of the Pugh Model of Design Boundaries provided in the introduction to this book, to determine how many of the cited 'design' and 'procurement' criteria were considered in the development of this government procurement card.

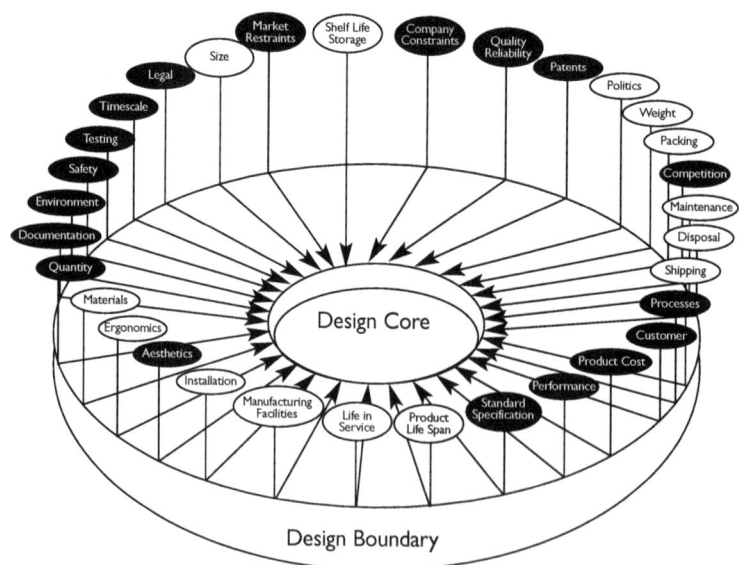

2. Consider how important the inclusion of these criteria is to the success of the entire project.

This contract was an innovative method of procuring small-value items that accumulated to considerable sums of money. The inclusion of the design criteria in the contract had a positive impact upon the ultimate contract. Some examples are provided here. The entire business was surrounded in security considerations that were of paramount importance to the ultimate procurement. Ultimately the government were buying a service, so the design of the attributes of this service is those that are explored in the case. The roll out of the service had to be planned carefully and was as much a part of the design of the work as the nature of the service itself.

The criteria identified above (question one) are important for various reasons. The documentation to procure the service and the nature of the documentation that formed part of the service was of vital importance if the government departments where to be able to record expenditure and crosscheck expenditure against the monthly statement received. The government cost accounting system demanded the transfer of expenditure into budget accounts. As the system had to be designed to pay all procurement cards centrally the method of transfer and recording that transfer was important.

The performance of the service was designed in such a way as to allow maximum flexibility to the users but maintained a level of control upon the user and the card to ensure that government was protected against fraudulent use of the card.

Market restraints operated in so far as the main institutions offered the government procurement card service under strict regulation and control. Specific banks operated under each institution and there was therefore a limited number of banks that could offer the service. The central institution backing the cards dictated the categories for expenditure. These could be limited or offered in their entirety by the individual government that proved to cause problems in the identification of the various expenditures.

Company constraints too had an impact upon the service choice and the flexibility of the use of the government procurement card.

3. **Identify the various stakeholders in this case study and explain the role that they played in the development of the final framework.**

- Procurement function of Department of Trade and Industry: who were responsible for the development of the requirement and the establishing of the contract.
- HM Treasury: who were central to the development of the initial concept of using the procurement card to buy goods and services within government.
- Visa, Master Card etc: these institutions proved instrumental in the design of the service offered to the government buyers.
- Consultants: who where involved in the surveys of government expenditure to assist in the planning of the implementation strategy for the use of the cards in the various government departments and agencies.
- Banks: who where involved with the design of the individual cards for the departments and in the design of how payment would be catered for in the service delivery.
- The card users: who were consulted during the trial to determine the selection of categories and the method of organisation of the service required to run the system on a wider scale.
- The auditors: who validated the system from a security point of view for the government.
- Suppliers: who were involved in the change of the system of ordering and invoicing from government departments which also required considerable change for the supplier in this aspect.

Case Study – Driving Theory Test – Driving Standards Agency

Case Synopsis

This case study represents the development of a major contract with the DSA for a new method of delivery of the theory element of the British driving test. It has been developed with members of the procurement team at the DSA. The case begins with a historical development of the circumstances leading up to the introduction of a separate theory test to the standard driving test process in the UK. European legislation is cited as a main driver for the development of the contract. The case explains the situation from 1994 through 2000 and the changes that took place to the theory test over that period. A highly complex process for setting test questions and ensuring both fairness and equity in the development of them from an educational perspective was only part of the contract procedure discussed. A very complex procedure is described whereby the process of applying for a theory test appointment through to eventually receiving test results and certificate passing the test and driving licence has been developed. All manner of considerations had to be taken into account such as psychological aspects to developing technologically based tests and how the candidates would react to these, along with delivering an effective and efficient system of delivering a good test-sitting experience is explained. This contract is a critically strategic contract to the DSA and has been successful in terms of enhanced revenue streams for the organisation, but more importantly it is a model approach to incorporating design criterion early in the procurement process and involving key stakeholders in the entire process. The case describes some key lessons learnt during the course of the contract development that show an enlightened procurement team and one that is geared to continually improve its performance.

The Approach Taken

The case has been written with full cooperation of the DSA Procurement Team. The case was approached from the perspective of design issues and how they had or had not been incorporated into the procurement strategy of an ICT-based procurement. It was particularly interesting to see how external factors such as behaviour and reaction of individuals affected the development of the computerised system along with the availability of products of this nature and suppliers for it in the market place. The full approach in terms of questioning and method has been incorporated into the chapter of introduction in this text. The Pugh Model of Design Boundaries has been used to identify the main elements considered in new product design and those most pertinent to criteria for making decisions for various procurements throughout both the private and public sectors. This model was identified at the end of the interview with a representative from DSA's Procurement Team, who have design considerations and procurement criteria in firm view when procurement work is undertaken in the organisation.

Teaching and Learning Objectives

- To provide students with the opportunity to study a case relaying best practice in the public sector procurement arena that explicitly incorporates ICT design concepts and complex service delivery parameters early in its procurement strategy.
- To help students understand areas of synergy between design criteria for the development of new products and the procurement criteria for the development of sound procurement decisions.
- To provide scope to track and analyse the design issues considered in the development of an ICT system.
- To examine the effect of design on procurement strategies.
- To explore the importance of involving key stakeholders in the procurement process throughout.

Main Issues Raised

- Consideration of design concepts
- Consideration of the impact of design upon the identification of need
- Consideration of design upon the finished procurement contract
- Consideration of procurement decision criteria
- Consideration of the value of procurement research
- Consideration of key elements of strategic procurement
- Consideration of the importance of external and internal interface in the development of the requirement for procurement.

Specific Questions

1. **Consider the development of the theory test from 1994 through 2000 in terms of procurement process and design issues by tracking the number and nature of issues that had to be incorporated into the overall project.**

Students should track through the process to determine the issues incorporated in the contract:

- European legislation
- Highway code
- Tendering regulations
- Coordination of practical and theory test examination
- Complexity of the specification for the theory test at first on paper and then on screen
- Numbers of potential suppliers of the service
- Conflict of interest
- Educational aspects of test development

- Writing questions for the test
- Design of method of managing the test centres
- Ergonomics
- Electronic marking system/ machinery
- Design of test paper
- Aesthetics
- Languages
- Inclusiveness of all potential users: techno-phobes, disabled, academically below average, foreign language speakers etc.
- Booking methods and payment management
- Costs
- Geographical location of test centres
- Standards and performance measures
- Invigilation and process management
- Association with driving licence
- Customer satisfaction
- Standards
- Accessibility
- Educational ability
- ICT performance on tests.

2. **Discuss the importance of the early inclusion of these issues to the success of the entire project.**

Given such a wide list of aspects that needed to be designed into the contract for driving theory tests the early inclusion of design criteria and principles is vital to the entire process. Students should explore each of the issues identified above to determine its impact upon the contract that was let. Of particular importance to the contract is the recognition of the need to consider academic ability, accessibility and the entire ICT testing process capacity to the onscreen test.

3. **Consider the DSA case study in the light of the Pugh Model of Design Boundaries provided in the introduction to this book, to determine how many of the cited 'design' and 'procurement' criteria were considered in the development of these ICT and service delivery contracts.**

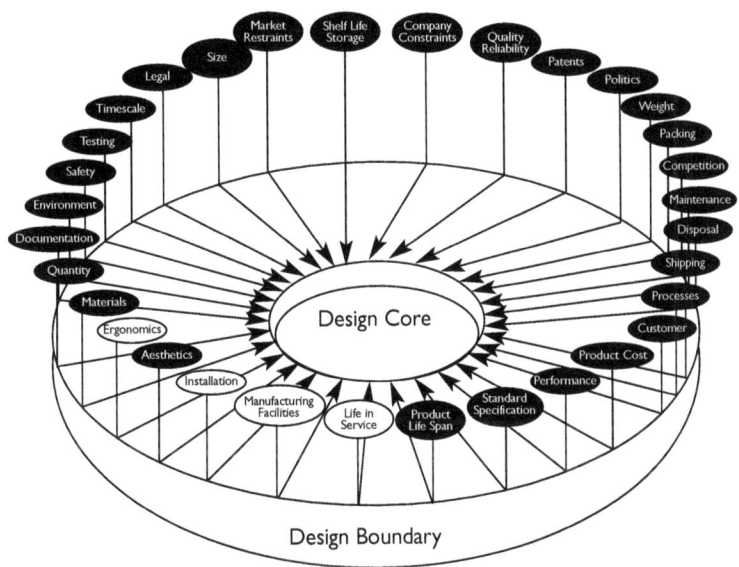

4. **Identify the stakeholders, their involvement and explain what impact their non-involvement might have had on the success of the project.**

There are many stakeholders involved to varying degrees. Each played their part in the design of this theory test product as it changed from paper-based to an ICT based contract.

- European Union: this body was involved in developing the legislation that prompted the contract.

- Department of the Transport and the Regions: this department of government is ultimately responsible for the contract.
- Driving Standards Agency: they are responsible for the coordination of the design of the theory test and its background support systems.
- Road Safety Division: who have been involved in the provision of information on road usage and accident rates etc which helped to target the policy on driving safety in UK.
- NFER: the body that is responsible for the development of the test questions and for the validation of the test questions.
- Suppliers: who are responsible for delivery of the service and thus have a role in the design and development of that service especially those tasked with the design of the test centre management and administration.
- National Audit Office: who played the part in the validation of the system of test provision for the DSA.
- Driving instructors: who had a part to play in the design of the service and had a vested interest in the new test approach.
- Parents and learners: who are identified as the main customers for the theory test and have been taken into account in the design and development of the test as part of an inclusion policy for all types of road user.
- Examination Award Body: responsible for the validation of the test questions to ensure that they are of an appropriate standard to meet the need of the theory test.
- Advisors: these bodies such as those in Australia demonstrated their computerised software system designed to offer tests on computer and through the medium of ICT.
- Ministers of Parliament: who played a roll in the lobbying for the test to be paper-based and then to enhance it to on-screen.

Case Study – DVLA-Vehicle Licensing Disc

Case Synopsis

This case study has been developed with the help of the procurement team at the DVLA based in Swansea in S. Wales. The case study examined the development of the contract to make Vehicle Excise Duty Discs (VEDD) that by law must be purchased either bi-annually or annually and displayed by all vehicle owners in Great Britain as a method of collection of government tax to pay for the use of the roads. This contract for VEDD is a core activity for the Agency, as it provides the visual display mechanism, in vehicles, of road drivers' compliance with the road traffic and taxation laws in Great Britain. This contract therefore has a very high profile for the Agency and design is of paramount importance in the development process. This particular contract exercise is still being effectively managed through its third year. The study begins with an explanation of the aims of the DVLA itself and follows the progress of the design of the specification and the support chain behind it. The case study begins with the procurement team about to begin the European tendering process. A dual-sourced approach is taken to permit backup for the supply of VEDD because of the importance of the contract product and to signify the criticality of supply of VEDD to the agency and the government too. The design of the disc is discussed revealing that the most important factors lie with the security of the development of the discs so as to avoid as much as possible the possibility of fraud or counterfeit. There are many stakeholders involved in the process ranging from the police and traffic wardens to the post office and vehicle registration offices through to the end customer, members of the British public. A strong reliance upon the suppliers and of course on their suppliers must be recognised, as there are various elements to the contract such as the design, paper, ink dye, printing, storage, transportation and distribution.

The contract has been managed well and the DVLA are rightly proud of the progress that has been made with the contract. They have been open about the lessons learnt and where they sought to improve the contract from the earlier sole sourced model previous used for the procurement of VEDD.

The Approach Taken

The case was approached from the perspective of design issues and how they have been integrated into the procurement strategy of this contract within DVLA. The full approach in terms of questioning and method has been incorporated into the chapter of introduction in this text. The Pugh Model of Design Boundaries has been used to identify the main elements considered in new product design and those most pertinent to criteria for making decisions for various procurements throughout both the private and public sectors. This model was described at the outset of the interview for the collection of data for this case study. It was also discussed throughout the case study research to help identify the extent to which the design and procurement factors mesh together in the development of a new product where the innovation of suppliers is required to ensure that the end product is suitable for the purpose designated for it.

Teaching and Learning Objectives

- To provide students with the opportunity to a case study that considers complex design issues early and throughout the procurement process.
- To help students understand areas of synergy between design criteria for the development of new products and the procurement criteria for the development of sound procurement decisions.
- To provide scope to analyse the design issues considered in the development of a vehicle licence contract.
- To explore the importance of involving key stakeholders in the procurement process throughout.

Main Issues Raised

- Consideration of design concepts
- Consideration of the impact of design upon the identification of need
- Consideration of design upon the finished procurement contract
- Consideration of procurement decision criteria
- Consideration of key elements of strategic procurement
- Consideration of the importance of external and internal interface in the development of the requirement for procurement
- Consideration of the impact of organisational values, mission and culture upon procurement decisions
- Consideration of supplier/buyer relationships
- Consideration of issues such as intellectual property rights and legal factors in the development of procurement contracts.

Specific Questions

1. Consider the DVLA Vehicle Excise Duty Disc case study in the light of strategic procurement planning and how design has featured in that planning.

DVLA have been forward thinking in the design of a seemingly small or insignificant item such as the Vehicle Licence Disc. Due the purpose of the disc there are many unexpected design issues that need to be built into the procurement contract for both the product development and the service behind it. Design issues such as security and safety in the disc, which plays a large part in the design of the disc using various overlapping measures to ensure that it is almost impossible to copy. Similarly the importance of the product to the government revenue and the legality of the drivers in the UK mean that the design of the product and the service in terms of timing, delivery, and accuracy are all key considerations. Aesthetics of the disc are important for several reasons as the discs are used by many of the authoritarian bodies to verify the legality of the vehicle displaying the disc. Visibility, size, colour and legibility are key design issues. If these matters are included in the design severe consequences for the entire country would arise. Individuals could not legally drive their cars and the revenue for the government would significantly diminish.

2. **Pugh's Model of Design Boundaries provided in the introduction to this book, cited 'design' and 'procurement' criteria that should be considered in the development of a new product. Consider how important the inclusion of these criteria is to the success of the entire project.**

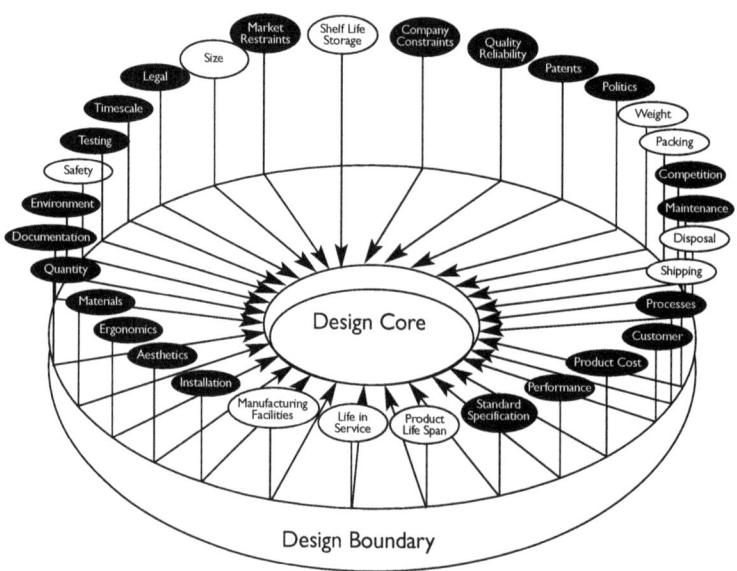

3. **Identify the involvement of the various stakeholders in this case study process and explain the role that they played in the development of its final framework.**

There are several key players in the design of the discs and the process of sale and despatch:

- European Union: dictating legislation on how the disc should look across Europe.
- DETR: who have the ultimate responsibility on behalf of government for the design and management of the VEDD.
- DVLA: Agency for the DETR responsible solely for the management of registration and licensing for vehicles
- DVLA Procurement Team: the managers of the contract and the key players in ensuring the designs and support systems meet the requirement.
- DVLO: responsible for the issue of driver licences and VEDD on a local basis.
- Police: who utilise the disc in law enforcement and who have played a role in the design of the disc itself.
- Traffic wardens: who utilise the discs as part of their law enforcement role and have a part to play in identifying the best position for the disc to be placed for identification purposes.
- Post office counters: who are involved in the control and sale of the discs to members of the public.
- Suppliers: who have played a major role in the design of the security controls and the appearance of the discs etc. They must organise stringent control measures for the packaging and distribution of the discs.
- New car salesrooms: the process has been changed in respect of distribution of discs through new car dealers due to their specific lobbying for a quicker method of obtaining VEDD for new cars that they sell.
- MOT garages: who are responsible for the crosscheck between the standard of repair of the vehicle and the legality to drive the vehicle on the roads of GB.
- Drivers: whilst the drivers have had little influence upon the design of the disc itself they have had an influence on the method of

procurement identified as acceptable for them to obtain the VEDD to be legally able to drive their cars.

Case Study – County Councils Waste Management

Case Synopsis

This case study identifies issues for consideration in the design of future contracts for the procurement of cleaning services for the purpose of waste management on local authority streets and domestic homes in the council area of East Abbeyworth in England. The case is put forward as a design and 'environmentally friendly' approach to the procurement of cleaning services. Students are invited to identify the design issues and comment upon how they might be addressed and on how they could impact the development of the service design to ensure that the council concerned meets all of the responsibilities. The approach to this matter follows an initiative across all county councils to ensure that the development of such contracts remains within government guidelines for the environmental procurement of materials and services pertinent to the cleaning services task. Waste management issues occupy a prominent place in the council business.

The Approach Taken

The case was approached from the perspective of design issues and how they have been integrated into the procurement strategy of this contract within the East Abbeyworth County Council. The full approach in terms of questioning and method for the development of the case study has been incorporated into the chapter of introduction in this text. The Pugh Model of Design Boundaries has been used to identify the main elements considered in new product design and those most pertinent to criteria for making decisions for various procurements throughout both the private and public sectors. This model was described at the outset of the interview for the collection of data for this case study. It was also discussed throughout the case study research to help identify the extent to which the design and procurement factors mesh together in the development of a new product where the innovation of suppliers is required to ensure that the end product is suitable for the purpose designated for it.

The contractual approach taken to the services for waste management could not be mapped as the approach to the procurement was ceased in favour of a more strategic review and integrated plan being devised. Nevertheless, the study throws up some interesting design areas for consideration when developing a complex service contractual approach such as this.

Teaching and Learning Objectives

- To provide students with the opportunity to understand a complex case study requiring integrated design management early in its procurement strategy.
- To provide students with the basis for a discussion on the procurement path that should be taken and the importance of design to both the product, service and the supply chain behind it all.
- To explore the importance of involving key stakeholders in the procurement process throughout.

Main Issues Raised

- Consideration of design concepts
- Consideration of the impact of design upon the identification of need
- Consideration of procurement decision criteria

- Consideration of the importance of external and internal interface in the development of the requirement for procurement.

Specific Questions

1. **Consider how design factors will feature in the planning of strategic procurement.**

Waste management is an area that attracts little interest to most individuals until something goes wrong with the collection, management or disposal of rubbish. The case looks specifically at domestic waste management from the perspective of the Council's requirement to integrate the management of many different services. The need to integrate different services automatically requires the design of an programme of services however in this regard there are issues that make the planning more complex such as legal dimensions, health and safety, space utilisation etc that adds to the need to strategically design the entire programme. Within this procurement area there are many design factors that feature in the creation of a requirement for this contract.

2. **Pugh's Model of Design Boundaries provided in the introduction to this book, cited 'design' and 'procurement' criteria that should be considered in the development of new product. Consider how important the inclusion of these criteria is to the success of this entire service development project.**

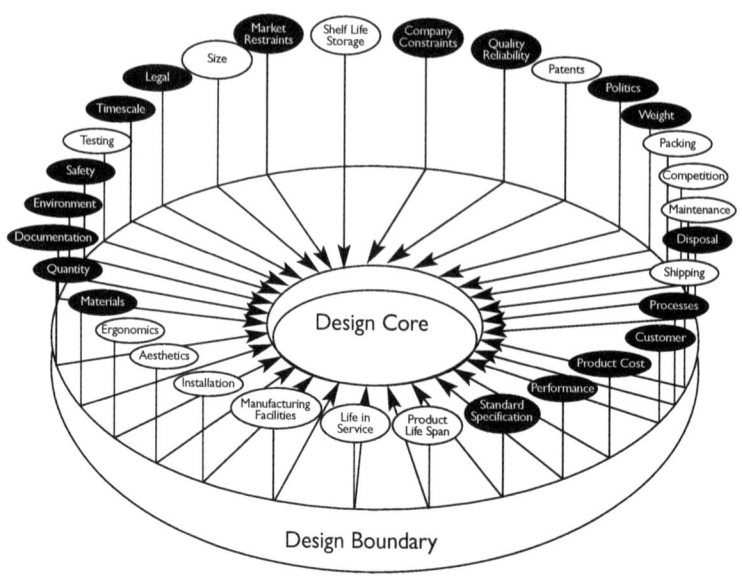

3. **Identify the involvement of the various stakeholders who could be in the case study and explain the role that they could play in the development of final framework.**

The management of waste for the County Council is a very important matter; here are some of the stakeholders who will have a roll:

- Government: who legislate on the way waste should be disposed of in the country.
- City Council procurement team who take the responsibility for the design and the development of the contract for waste management throughout the council
- City council councillors: who will act as both lobbyers in representation of their electors and as validators of the policy to dispose of the waste.
- Contractors: who will be employed for the purposes of disposing of the rubbish or managing the other identified waste disposal
- Householders: who create the waste but also insist on standards for removal of the waste management as taxpayers.

Bibliography

- Bagozzi, Richard P. 1975 'Marketing as Exchange', *Journal of Marketing* 39 (October).
- Beckwith D, Harris D, 1993 'The Megateam Design Process: Adding a new Dimension to Concurrent Development.' *Design Management Journal.*
- Butterworth - Heinemann Ltd. Vol. 11 No 4 Oct 90.
- Desbarats, Gus: May 1995 'Usability Form that says Function (product design)', *Industrial Management and Data Systems*. Volume 95.
- Faust W. 1993, 'Cross-functional Teams in Design: A case Study of Thermos Thermal Electric Grill', *Design Management Journal.*
- Francis A Fischbacher, M. 1997. 'Managing Service Sector Product Design.' Design Council Funded research.
- Gasser L. 1989. 'Designing Internal Communications Strategies: A Critical Organisational need.' *Employment Relations.*
- Heskett J. 1989. *'Philips :* A study of the Corporate Management of Design.'
- Hollins G & Hollins B, 1993 *Total Design – Managing the Design Process in the Service Sector*. Pitman Publishing.
- Hollins B, Pugh S. 1990. *Successful Product Design*, Butterworths.
- Hughes J, Cox A, Ralf M. 1997. 'Facilitating Strategic Change – the Key Role for Purchasing Leadership.' IPSERA Conference paper
- Jones JC, 1990. *Depending on everyone: some thoughts on contextual design*. Butterworth-Heinemann Ltd.
- Lamming R. & Cox A. *Strategic Procurement in the 1990's.*

- Lusch RF, Brown SW, Brunswick GJ, 'A General Framework for Explaining Internal Vs External Exchange.' *Journal of the Academy of Marketing Science*, Volume, 20, Number 2 pages p 119 -134

- Ostberg Gustaf. 1994. *What goes on when a designer thinks?* AI & Society 8:45 –87

- Saunders M, 1990. *Strategic Supply Chain Management*. The Chartered Institute of Purchasing and Supply. Pitman Publishers.

- Schneider E 1989. 'Unchaining the Value of Design.' *European Management Journal.*

- Smith Gerald E. Fall 1995 'Framing Product Design using Design communication to Facilitate User Learning.' *Journal of Business and Industrial Marketing.*

- Walsh V, Roy, R, Bruce M & Potter S. 1992 *Winning by Design, Design Innovation Group*. Blackwell Business Press. London.

- Wilson R, 'Service Design, A Scoping Study on the trend towards services and the issues of service design.' June 1998

www.ingramcontent.com/pod-product-compliance
Ingram Content Group UK Ltd.
Pitfield, Milton Keynes, MK11 3LW, UK
UKHW021320180426
11947UKWH00015B/1337